D0619448

Stewart,
Your book is a gem! Diamonds! Wish I had written it ... but then, you were my teacher! Thank you for ever.
Brother Andrew

It was my privilege to serve in the International Office of WEC under Stewart's incisive and courageous leadership – a leadership that enabled WEC to expand, develop and grow through major new advances to the least evangelized peoples of the earth. I commend this book as a means for equipping others with like vision.
Patrick Johnstone, author of *Operation World*.

Stewart Dinnen challenges us to find God's highest solution to our most down-to-earth difficulties.
Brian Woodford, WEC International Training and Resources Secretary

You Can
Learn To Lead

Stewart Dinnen

Christian Focus

By the same author
All For The Best
Faith on Fire
Here We Stand
How Are You Doing?
Rescue Shop Within a Yard of Hell
When I Say Move

© Stewart Dinnen
ISBN 1 857 92 824

Text initially prepared for the members of WEC International
by Stewart R. Dinnen, formerly International Secretary.

Published in 1997 by Christian Focus Publications, Geanies
House, Fearn, Ross-shire, IV20 ITW, Great Britain.

Reprinted 1998

Cover design by Donna Macleod

Printed and bound in Great Britain by
The Guernsey Press Co. Ltd., Guernsey, Channel Islands

Contents

Foreword

Here is a handbook on Christian leadership that comes from the front-line of mission endeavour. The vital issues raised, the condensed style, the real life illustrations, all reflect the burden of a mission leader who has been out in front pointing the way and urging us on for a whole generation.

Stewart Dinnen is an excellent teacher. First he inspires us to excellence, then he exposes our weaknesses and shows us the way forward. He doesn't preach. Instead he challenges us to find God's highest solutions to our most down-to-earth difficulties. As Stewart's introduction reminds us, this is not a book to be read at one sitting. Each chapter is virtually a course outline and will repay careful study.

Written primarily as a training manual for leaders of WEC International scattered over 50 nations, the examples are from our own Mission history – what God has taught us. Nevertheless, we are glad other missions organisations intend to make use of this unique resource. As God has so long used SRD among us, so we pray that this manual will be long used to strengthen the hands of yet another generation of leaders.

Brian Woodford
WEC International Training and Resources Secretary
Gerrards Cross
United Kingdom

EXPLANATORY NOTE

This book has been written at the request of WEC's International Office and with the support and encouragement of a number of WEC leaders.

It brings together the teachings on WEC leadership that were first produced in:

* WECMANAIR (WEC management airletter, 1975-83)
* THE INTERCON 84 STRATEGY PAPERS (1984-86)
* LIGHT ON LEADERSHIP (1988-89)
* THE INTERCON 90 LEADERSHIP SEMINAR
* LEADERSHIP LINK (1990-92)

Where the same topic has been touched upon in several issues the content has been synthesised and edited to give the best sequence of thought.

Occasionally, new material has been added where it was felt needed in order to clarify or develop an idea. The chapter on stress is new material prepared by request of the leaders' conference in 1990.

A set of questions has been added at the end of each chapter to stimulate thought and discussion.

It must be emphasised that, for a variety of reasons, the original text was written in a very 'compressed' style; therefore, the material should not be read speedily or continuously. The reader will gain most by taking in – at the very most – one chapter at a time and by reflecting on the issues raised so that they can be applied in practical ways.

It should also be remembered that the main reason for this manual was to re-present material already dealt with in letter or article form. It is not, therefore, intended to be a comprehensive treatment of all aspects of leadership.

The concept of this book was 'pioneered' in Indonesia by WEC missionary Jeff Gulleson, who arranged for the translation and distribution of selected material for the use of numerous Indonesian Christian leaders.

The writer was International Resources Secretary of WEC from 1979-83, then International Secretary from 1983-87.

An enormous debt of gratitude is owed to Diane Griffiths, a former WEC member, who has given dozens of hours on the word processor to bring this manuscript to readable form.

Bible references are from the NIV unless otherwise stated.

Stewart Dinnen
Tasmania
1993

SECTION I

CARE AND CONCERN

SERVANT	EXAMPLE	PASTOR	TEACHER/OVERSEER	COUNSELLOR	INTERCESSOR
ACTS 20					
I serve the Lord with humility (v. 19).	Keep watch over yourselves (v. 28)	Keep watch over all the flock (v. 28)	Be shepherds (feed) the church (v. 28) made overseers (v. 28)	I never stopped warning you (v. 31)	I commit you to God (v. 32) Knelt down and prayed (v. 36)
1 CORINTHIANS 3 and 4					
only servants (3:5). regard us as servants (4:1)	so that you may learn from us (4:6) imitate me (4:16)	I became your father through the gospel (4:15)	Which agrees with what I teach (4:17)	I am writing this to warn (counsel) you (4:14)	
COLOSSIANS 1 and 4					
I have become its servant (1:25)		so that we may present everyone perfect in Christ (1:28)	to present to you the word of God (1:25) teaching everyone (1:28)	Admonishing (counselling) everyone with all wisdom (1:28)	We pray for you (1:3) We have not stopped praying for you (1:9) Epaphras is always wrestling in prayer for you (4:12)

1

The Seven Roles of the Leader

What are the essential responsibilities of a leader? The Scriptures give us seven pictures: example, servant, pastor, teacher, overseer, counsellor and intercessor, and the purpose of this chapter is to identify the spiritual principles related to these, because each highlights a particular area of responsibility.

A 'panorama' is given on the opposite page. A selection of Biblical phrases under each heading seeks to substantiate the titles or roles specified.

Paul's 'leadership seminar' with the Ephesian church elders in Acts 20:17-37 makes a rich and rewarding study, and provides us with an excellent summary of his concepts of leadership.

From verse 28 we find example, pastoral care, teaching and overseeing. Servanthood is in verses 19 and 34; personal example is stressed in verses 18, 19, 24, 33-35; teaching comes in verses 20, 21, 25, 27, 31 and 32; counselling in verse 31, pastoral care in verse 35, and the intercessor's role in verse 36.

1. Servanthood

Some find it difficult to correlate leadership with servanthood, but it becomes easier when we take them at the level of values, attitudes and resources. It becomes easier still when we study the Lord's example in John 13 and His teaching in Matthew 20:28. We can see from these that *uppermost in His mind were the needs of those He was serving*, and His total commitment was to their welfare.

We will never do this in our own strength, but when we accept the Cross as a principle it becomes the key to our lifestyle.

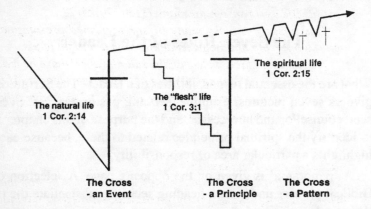

The first part of the diagram represents the downward drift of the unregenerate person, until he becomes aware of the efficacy of Christ's death. Through repentance and faith he is born again and starts walking the heavenward track.

But most Christians, after a while, realise that there is a civil war raging in the heart. Independent self (the flesh) is at variance with the spirit, until the Cross principle is accepted. ('Not I, but Christ'.) Jesus makes it clear that true discipleship is only possible after we accept the Cross (Luke 14:27, Matt. 10:38).

The final part of the diagram represents life in the Spirit. The dips in the line are meant to represent the reality of our imperfections, but by a daily application of the Cross we can keep short accounts with the Lord, accept His discipline and keep on growing.

One of the best commentaries on servant-style leadership comes in *A Theology of Church Leadership* by L. Richards and C. Holdtke.

You know that the rulers of the Gentiles lord it over them, and their high officials exercise authority over them. Not so with you. Instead, whoever wants to become great among you must be your servant, and whoever wants to be first must be your slave – just as the Son of Man did not come to be served, but to serve, and to give his life as a ransom for many (Matt. 20:25-28).

This passage attacks many of our ingrained presumptions about leadership and helps us define how a servant leads.

The passage states it clearly: the ruler is 'over' those he leads. But the servant is 'among'. We cannot be servant-leaders if our position or role or our own attitude tends to lift us above others and makes a distinction between us and the rest of the people of God.

Authority-style Leadership
Command authority tells others what to do. The leadership mode involves issuing orders, passing on decisions the leader has made. Servants have one role in the household – to serve. Rather than tell, the servant shows. Example, not command, is the primary mode through which the servant leads.

The command authority of the secular ruler does lead to behavioural change. There are all sorts of sanctions that secular leaders – be they in the military, in government, or in business – rely on to obtain the behaviour they require. But servants must rely on an inner response in those they influence. Without the power to coerce behaviour, servants must seek the free choice of the ones being led. The one style achieves behavioural conformity; the other style achieves heart commitment.

The qualities of a servant leader

a. Humility (Acts 20:19)
b. Meekness, Gentleness (2 Tim. 2:24,25)
c. Devotion to those he serves (John 10:15)
d. Motivated for their highest good (Phil. 2:20)
e. Cares for those he serves (1 Thess. 2:7)

f. Anticipates needs (1 Cor. 16:2)

g. Faithful (1 Cor. 4:1,2)

h. Diligent (2 Tim. 4:2)

i. Doesn't argue (2 Tim. 2:24)

j. Not a 'person pleaser' (1 Tim. 6:17,18)

k. Serves as 'unto the Lord' (1 Cor. 2:1-5)

l. Not fearful of consequences of a right decision (1 Cor. 4:2)

m. Serves with joy (2 Cor. 6:10)

n. Vulnerable (2 Cor. 12:9)

o. Doesn't wear a mask (1 Thess. 2:5)

p. Prayerful for those he serves (Phil. 1:3-6)

q. Impartial (1 Tim. 5:21)

Was Paul a 'servant leader'?
   Answer:
     'What is Apollos? What is Paul? Only servants' (1 Cor. 3:5).
     'Men ought to regard us as servants' (Col. 1:23).
     'Paul, a servant' (Rom. 1:1, Phil. 1:1, Tit. 1:1).

Both by example and precept a certain regional base leader became known for his servant spirit. His position was that sending base workers were there to meet the needs of overseas workers, especially when they were on home leave. His great delight was to be a taxi-driver, tea-maker and meeting organiser for them. Everyone loved to go to his area!

2. Example

Example or 'modelling' is perhaps the most potent means of influencing others. We are all made with a capacity for imitation, and it is one of the simplest forms of teaching.

We could say that this is the truth underlying the incarnation of the Lord Jesus. His life was a revelation of the nature of God; it was also a pattern of perfect human behaviour.

So too with Paul. Remember that the Gospels had not been

written, so he encouraged imitation of himself and his way of life (1 Cor. 4:16, 11:1; Phil. 3:17, 4:9; 1 Thess. 1:6; 2 Thess. 3:7,9).

Why is testimony so important? It is the basis and ground of our standing before others. If we are not held in respect we will not have followers!

In communication theory the power of the 'para-message' is well known. (The para-message is the message-beside-the-message; it is the informal impact of our own personality, the effect of our testimony.)

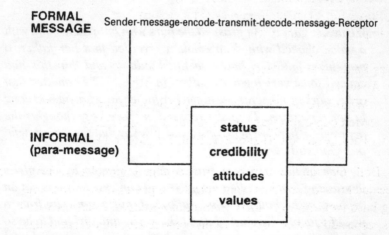

FORMAL MESSAGE Sender-message-encode-transmit-decode-message-Receptor

INFORMAL (para-message)

status
credibility
attitudes
values

Note how the synagogue audience responds to the teaching of Jesus. 'All were amazed at the gracious words that came from his lips' (response to the formal message). 'Isn't this Joseph's son?' they asked (response to the informal message).

The key to effective modelling is the degree to which the model is willing to identify with the followers and to open up to them in honesty and reality. An admission of vulnerability or failure does not ruin one's status – it actually enhances it.

In an article entitled 'Self-exposure – the bridge to fellowship' published in *Practical Anthropology*, Mar-Apr 1965, Jacob Loewen writes:

If we really want to enter into any intimate relationship with other human beings there is a way: the way of self-exposure. We will have to be willing to be known, if we want to know. Self-exposure will be of utmost importance to the missionary, for it will reveal in real life his encounter with the doctrines he is teaching. Values are always best taught in the drama of life, not in preaching.

He goes on to give an example of this in a prison service taken by a group of his students. One of the girls was asked to give her testimony.

When she got up, she grasped the bars with both hands and with a voice choked with deep emotion revealed that her father, a prominent minister, had committed suicide and that this had caused some very intense conflicts in her life. She admitted that in her darker moments she hated her father for what he had done to her reputation. Then she realised in those very thoughts the depravity of her own heart and could only say that she was grateful that God still cared for her.

One of the prisoners was so deeply shaken by the girl's unmasking that he called the jailer and confessed he was not an orphan, as he had previously affirmed, but a runaway from a wealthy family. He said, 'I don't know why that girl had to be so honest.' The young man was reunited with his family and later his sentence was suspended because of the transformation that had taken place in his life.

3. Pastor

Pastoral care is often the key in effective leadership today. The older generation of missionaries did not expect or receive much in the way of pastoral care, but today's generation expects it and feels cheated if it is not given. So the leader, who is often a member of a generation older than the group he is leading, needs to make a special effort here.

It is interesting that the Lord Jesus describes Himself in John 10 as the good shepherd (11,14), the knowledgeable shepherd (14,27), the sacrificial shepherd (11,15), the life-giving shepherd (10,28), the protective shepherd (10,29), the seeking shepherd (16).

The writer of the Hebrews describes him as 'that great Shepherd' (13:20).

The field leader of one of WEC's large fields was held in high respect by his team. The reason: he and his wife gave themselves to regular consistent visitation of every team member. Although by gifting an evangelist, this had a low priority compared with his pastoral ministry.

Another leader on a different field chose to locate himself a considerable distance from the majority of workers. Pastoral care was minimal because of the sheer logistics involved.

This subject requires special treatment and is taken up in Chapter 2.

4. Teacher

Leaders will find themselves more readily accepted if they can show that they have a good grasp of spiritual principles and can relate them effectively to lives and situations. It is impossible to take others further than one has personally travelled, spiritually. If we have the truth and experience we will speak with recognisable authority.

What is our goal as teacher-leaders?

a. To impart the knowledge of relevant spiritual truth.

b. To pray for enlightenment and understanding of those for whom we are responsible.

c. To challenge the will to apply the truth in life.

A leader also needs to accept the responsibility for the further training of those in his care. He may be able to provide this himself (one field leader ran a course in homiletics for members of his team who had weak communication skills), or he may recommend books, resources or courses which can be taken. He should have a goal of encouraging team members to improve their capacities and skills.

One sending base leader called in his key men for a five-day seminar on how to run a course on 'mission perspectives'. This is now being offered to churches. A similar course run in another sending base has resulted in many young people moving into training.

Study the lives of the great leaders in the Bible and you will find references to their ministry of teaching.

Moses	These are the commands ... the LORD directed me to teach you (Deut. 6:1).
Samuel	I will teach you the way that is good and right (1 Sam. 12:23).
The Lord Jesus	The crowds were amazed at his teaching (Matt. 7:28).
	If anyone loves me, he will obey my teaching (John 14:23).
Paul	Hold to the teachings we passed on to you (2 Thess. 2:15).
	The commission of God ... to present to you the word of God in its fulness (Col. 1:25).
Peter	Jesus said [to Peter], 'Feed my lambs' (John 21:15).
	I will always remind you of these things ... it is right to refresh your memory (2 Pet. 1:12-13).

It was said of the Lord that He 'taught as one who had authority and not as their teachers of the law'.

What made the difference?

Answer: He was the embodiment of all He was teaching.

5. Overseer

The key concept in overseeing is discovering the direction in which the team needs to move. It is here that the leader functions as a visionary. His role is to discern the leading of the Spirit and to encourage team members in that direction. This is not to say that team members have no responsibility for discerning the Lord's mind, but it is pre-eminently the leader's task to be up-front in discovering the course which the team should take.

So the leader should develop a style of leadership that gives him time and room to be alone with God. Beware of the pressures (yes, the tyranny) of the urgent. There will always be pressure to be *doing*. But God's man will ensure he is in a position to be *hearing* and *seeing* what the Spirit is saying.

Note that when Paul's team was in a quandary in Troas, it was he who stayed up at night for prayer and waiting on God. That gave the Spirit the opportunity to impart the vision of the man of Macedonia (who turned out to be a woman – Lydia).

The secret of WEC's amazing growth in the fifties and sixties was Norman Grubb's capacity for leading the staff and candidates in the daily two-hour morning 'devotions' towards the discovery of the strategy of the Spirit, and his ability to minister faith and vision in facing the challenge of the unevangelised.

6. Counsellor

a. An inevitable responsibility

The WEC leader will constantly be called upon for advice. This will be particularly so during the early years of new workers; his knowledge, ministry expertise, experience, and his understanding of cultural norms will be invaluable assets to team members.

The factor that will limit effectiveness in this area is his busyness. If workers perceive him to be constantly under pressure they will not approach him except in dire emergencies.

The key in counselling is *accurate diagnosis*. We can give relevant advice only when we are fully conversant with the problem. This comes down to attentive listening.

For an example of effective listening, diagnosis and counselling, study the conversation between Jesus and the Samaritan woman (John 4:7-26), and the outcome (vv. 28-30, 39-42).

b. How to be a good listener

- Concentrate on what is currently being said rather than on wondering how to reply.
- Sit still. Give undivided attention.
- Listen with your *eyes*. Watch body language (eye and facial movements, body posture, gestures, etc.).
- Encourage the counsellee with responsive phrases ('I understand', 'I see', 'Good').
- Ask the right questions to fill in blanks of knowledge. Avoid questions that result in yes/no answers. Rather say, 'How would you describe your attitude when ...'
- Don't start to give advice without having all the needed information.
- Listen for feelings as well as facts. Expressing feelings helps to de-fuse the speaker. (A further help to de-fusing is to describe his feelings back to him but in different words.)
- Accept what people say without necessarily agreeing with them.
- Avoid a judgmental attitude. (Be careful with the question 'Why?')

Don't give advice if you really need time to think. Ask the counsellee to call back, if necessary.

The writer still has vivid memories of sessions with Norman Grubb in which he just sat quietly, giving an encouraging nod now and then. There was a sense that he hadn't a concern in the world other than fully understanding one's problem.

7. Intercessor

The intercessor's characteristics are:

a. Responsibility (Exod. 32:32)

The true intercessor receives a commission from the Lord for another person or situation and he carries this as a responsibility until that commission is withdrawn. Moses felt this for the Children of Israel and as a result offered to forfeit his life if this would bring God's forgiveness to the people.

b. Intensity (Col. 4:12)

Epaphras carried out his intercessory role with intensity. 'Wrestling' is from the Greek word *agonizomai* from which our word 'agonise' comes.

c. Identification (Rom. 9:3)

Paul was so burdened and identified with his fellow Jews that he was willing to be 'accursed from God' if it would result in the Jews' salvation.

d. Continuity (Exod. 17:11)

The key to the outcome of the battle with the Amalekites was Moses' willingness to continue in uninterrupted intercession, signified physically by the arms constantly raised.

e. Accountability (Heb. 13:17)

Leaders are here encouraged to maintain a watch-care ministry for the flock because God holds them accountable for the spiritual state of the members.

f. Authority (Acts 16:18)

From the pattern of Christ's encounter with demonic forces and from the example of Paul here, there is an inescapable obligation for us to confront, and assert our authority over, the forces of darkness.

g. Strategy (Isa. 40:31)

Intercession, to be truly effective, must be within the confines of the strategy of the Spirit. This was the key element in the intercession of the young church in Acts 4:29, 30. 'Now, Lord, consider their threats [the opposition of the enemy] and enable your servants to speak your word ... Stretch out your hand to heal and perform miraculous signs...'

A retired missionary of another mission approached the writer some years back. 'Brother, you are carrying big responsibilities in the work of the Lord and the Holy Spirit has told me I am to be one of your intercessors.' He has carried this ever since (and is now 84).

The Scriptures frequently couple the leader's role with that of the intercessor, e.g.

- In the life of Moses: Exod.3, 9:29, 14:15, 17:4, 19:20, etc.
- In the life of Samuel: 1 Sam.7, 1 Sam.12.
- In the life of Paul: Rom.1:9-10, 9:3, Phil.1:3,4,9, Col.1:3,9, 1 Thess.1:2-3, etc.

A leader without a systematic prayer ministry for his workers misses one of the most vital components of his commission.

Questions for study and discussion

1. Of the seven roles listed on pp. 8-21, in which do you perform best? Which is your weakest? What can be done about the weakest?

2. How do the fruits of the Spirit relate to leadership? How do the gifts of the Spirit relate to leadership?

3. Is there a difference between the authority of a church leader and the authority of a mission leader?

4. How can the servant-leader rightfully avoid becoming a door-mat?

5. 'They keep watch over you' (Heb. 13:17 NIV). 'They watch for your souls' (KJV). What does this mean for you? What should it mean?

Bibliography

E. Dayton & T. Engstrom, *The Christian Executive* (Waco, TX: Word Books, 1979)

T. Engstrom, *The Making of a Christian* (Grand Rapids, MI: Zondervan, 1976)

P. Greenslade, *Leadership* (Basingstoke, Hants: Marshall, 1984)

A. Le Peau, *Paths of Leadership* (London, UK: Scripture Union, 1983)

L. Richards & C. Hoeldtke, *A Theology of Church Leadership* (Grand Rapids, MI: Zondervan, 1980)

J. O. Sanders, *Spiritual Leadership* (London, UK: Marshall, Morgan & Scott, 1967)

2

Pastoral Care

An observation

After a visit to ten fields and five sending bases in '81-82, the then International Resources Secretary observed:

> *The happiest fields are those where* sensitive leadership *exists – sensitivity to workers' aspirations, ideas, gifts and potential on the one hand, and to their hang-ups, limitations and needs on the other. When workers sense that their leader* cares *all sorts of hardships and problems can be cheerfully gone through. When workers sense indifference and insensitivity, and when their leaders do not visit them for months on end, they often feel neglected, discouraged and out on a limb.*

A couple on a certain sending base were being considered for leadership. They had been functioning as acting-leaders for the previous year. One worker remarked: 'They even phoned round to ask us how we were! That's the first time a leader has done that with me during the ten years I've been in WEC.'

1. The leader is a pastor

Like it or not the simple truth is that a major component of WEC leadership is *pastoral care*. The reasons for this are:

a. Other sources of pastoral care and concern are not likely to exist, or are too distant for them to be available in any practical sense.

b. The leader is the most mature person to turn to, in view of his experience and understanding of workers' situations and background.

c. The leader is likely to be in a somewhat older age-bracket and would therefore be expected to bring a degree of wisdom and maturity to any counsel given.

d If the workers' problems involve relations with nationals, again the leader is the usual liaison person, because of his link with the national church and knowledge of the culture.

On the other hand the leader has his limitations:

e. He may come from a sending base and culture very different from the worker needing help.

f. Like it or not, the leader is an 'authority figure' in the situation, and the worker may be reticent to share for that very reason.

g. Any advice given, as an authority figure, is bound to be considered 'official' and binding.

h. If the worker's problem involves his relationship to authority, the leader starts at a disadvantage because the worker will not consider his views as being objective and neutral.

2. How can a leader's capacity for pastoral care be enhanced?

a. Firstly by understanding that all leaders naturally gravitate to one of two directions – *concentration on work* or *concentration on people*. (See Chapter 4 for further explanation.) The one who naturally concentrates on work needs to seek the Lord for special grace, and quite deliberately immerse himself in 'people situations' (in which he will not naturally feel at home) so as to expose himself to personal issues and gain sensitivity through interaction. This will require conscious effort.

b. Cultivate a ministry of intercession on behalf of your team members. There is nothing like prayer for bringing us into an attitude of concern, appreciation and love for people. And as we go over their strengths and weaknesses before the Lord, the Holy Spirit will put a divine compassion into our hearts.

c. Cultivate a spirit of holy enquiry into their well-being. This must stop short of inquisitiveness and high pressure tactics, but it should be an objective of every visit that the right questions (hopefully prepared beforehand) be asked and answers obtained.

For some workers their problem areas are immediately apparent but for others it requires a high degree of patience, restraint and discernment to discover what the problem issues really are.

Have some pre-determined areas to think about, e.g.

- Family relationships (or lack of them, for single people).
- Children's education, health and development.
- Accommodation.
- Eating/food.
- Emotional stability.
- Adaptation to culture.
- Finance, support level.
- Physical.
- Relationship with others – missionaries/nationals.
- Effectiveness in ministry.
- Language proficiency.
- Transport/vehicle.
- Spiritual factors – prayer, etc.
- Concerns about distant family – children or parents at home.

d. Be determined to be more than a leader. Let your goal be that you will so conduct yourself that you will be respected, yes, loved, as a brother or sister in Christ, a fellow prayer-partner, a good friend, an understanding co-worker.

e. Trust God to give you skills as an encourager. This is a great ministry, and a detailed study of the life of Barnabas will bring great rewards.

Encouragement involves:

- a positive attitude ('but Barnabas took him ...').

- an understanding of the worker's goals.

- an ability to reinvigorate others' desires to achieve personal and team goals.

- an ability to identify sources of discouragement and to deal effectively with them.

- a loving recognition and affirmation of the individual's abilities and potentials.

- a grasp of spiritual warfare and a capacity to resist and bind the enemy's attacks on the individual.

- an ability to recognise low self-image and administer the antidote – 'Christ in you, the hope of glory'.

f. Ask God to give you discernment in recognising the individual's spiritual gifts. This will lead on to ensuring that the individual has a task commensurate with these.

A young worker, ministering at a sending base annual staff conference, lost his train of thought, couldn't get started again, so sat down. During the tea break following he was seen sneaking off on his own, obviously feeling he was an abject failure. But another worker stopped him. 'Don't feel condemned because you didn't finish. What you did say was a real blessing!' In a moment the drooping shoulders were squared again and a new light came into his face.

3. Pastoral care means feeding the flock

Although all workers should have the capacity to feed themselves it is the mark of a good pastor that he ensures the team gets spiritual nourishment. How can this be done?

a. By being ready to bring spiritual principles into talks with individuals.

b. By bringing spiritual truths into letters.

c. By having an intra-field letter that includes a segment that ministers to spiritual needs.

d. By having a circulating folder/folders in which valuable articles that you have benefitted from can be a blessing to others.

e. By recommending relevant books and cassettes.

f. By building up a good field library of useful resources. (Every worker going on home leave should be asked to bring two new books back for the library.)

g. By encouraging attendance at deeper-life conferences, conventions, seminars, etc. (Even plan them.)

h. By stimulating corporate prayer at every opportunity, during visits, at monthly meetings, days of prayer, and by planning a sizeable slot in field conferences.

i. By having a list of prayer topics in the intra-field newsletter.

4. In addition, pastoral care means aiming for these qualities:

a. Ability to identify, empathise, place oneself in another's shoes.

b. Ability to relate, have interaction, willingness to visit, spend time, in order to understand people and situations.

c. Capacity for active listening, attentiveness, concentration.

d. Acceptance, having a non-judgmental attitude.

e. Personal vulnerability – ability to project an image of one who is still learning and can make mistakes. Expressed fallibility.

f. Concern for the security and protection of another.

g. Ability to keep confidences, keep promises. Reliability as a counsellor.

h. Availability, approachability, accessibility.

i. Anticipatory ability to foresee and forestall crises, anticipate reactions, evaluate possible responses.

j. Ability to make an objective (neutral) assessment, not swayed by strong personalities.

k. Readiness to pray with others in their presence and pray for others in their absence (the intercessor's role).

l. Thoughtfulness for people not present. Expressed concern for them by letter, phone call, message.

m. Concern about others' situations, circumstances, family, ministry.

n. Readiness to give practical expression to care and concern, e.g. give hospitality, invite for meals, keep open home, arrange for help and provide relief if there is sickness, tension or some threat.

o. Capacity to 'hold to the highest' and uphold Biblical and Mission principles.

p. Ability to confront or challenge, in love, when it is needed.

Two workers located 300 miles from their sending base HQ were relating with amazement what had happened some weeks before. 'X (the leader) was on his way home having been away from his family for quite some time, but he came by and stayed with us for two whole days so he had a good grasp of our situation. He really *cares*!'

31

Questions for study and discussion

1. Study the life of Barnabas and draw up a list of his abilities.
   Acts 4:36; 9:27; 11:22-29; 13:1,13-14; 1 Cor. 9:6; Col. 4:10.

2. If a leader is not a "natural" pastor what can be done to compensate for this?

3. How does one retain a ministry of encouragement yet be able to confront, correct, or rebuke?

4. Compile a list of the components of *caring*, e.g.

   • Perception

   • Compassion

   • Empathy ...

Bibliography

L. Crabb, *Effective Biblical Counselling* (Grand Rapids, MI: Zondervan, 1984)

L. Crabb & D. Allender, *Encouragement, the Key to Caring* (Grand Rapids, MI: Zondervan, 1984)

N. Wakefield, *Listening* (Waco, TX: Word Books, 1981)

3

How to Avoid Resignations

Whatever the underlying causes for a resignation the leader is inevitably involved; or worse, implicated; or worse still, is the reason itself! Every resignation to some degree reflects on the managing and pastoring capacity of the leader.

1. How to reduce the likelihood of resignation

a. Maintain a vital pastoral caring interest in every worker. Do not be satisfied with a superficial knowledge of situations and people. Trust God for discernment so as to understand and be able to empathise with each worker. 'We get a foothold in human lives by naturalness, by humour, and by caring for people. We get leverage by knowing when to agree and when to disagree, and how to disagree.' (S. Shoemaker)

b. If a. is carried out, then you will not be taken unawares by a sudden resignation. In actual fact, while the actual writing of a resignation letter may take only a few minutes, the build-up to that point must often take months, even years. If the leader is doing his job he will be aware of tensions, underlying causes of friction, frustration, discouragement, despair, poor inter-personal relationship, overload, critical attitudes, marital problems, cultural maladjustment, stress, et cetera.

c. As an addendum to this chapter we supply the main reasons for resignation over a number of years.

Note that the main reasons are:

• Spiritual/emotional/temperamental.

• Disagreement with, or lack of commitment to, mission policy, leadership.

• Inability to find, develop or maintain a ministry.

It should be obvious that the quality of leadership is a major component in each of these three factors.

d. Make sure a 'safety valve' mechanism exists so that when pressure builds up on a worker, there is a ready and recognised system in place for the cause to be exposed and talked over with the leader.

It may be taken care of by the leader's regular and frequent visits, or by an agreement for every worker to visit base at regular intervals, or the ready availability of the leader's deputy or substitute as counsellor.

There should be absolutely no reason for a worker to feel shut off and out on a limb.

e. There are at least twelve things that workers consciously or unconsciously expect as members of a team. The list is given in Chapter 4. Check these carefully against what is actually happening in your team situation.

f. Often a worker will want to leave a particular ministry, but not leave the organisation. Make provision for this.

g. Ensure you have a 'Barnabas' ministry to every worker.

h. Try hard to understand prickly people. Major Mike Mansfield (leader of the mercenaries who rescued WEC missionaries in Zaire during the Simba rebellion) has written:

Some men are what I call 'prickly pears'. Frequently these men are tough and independent. A weak leader ... will avoid them altogether or give in to them. This is an error. You must recognise strength in a personality even though it makes your life harder. So often I have found these 'prickly pears' to be the ones who are still in there fighting when all others have fled for the basic reason that they are obstinate and will not give in. This priceless quality ... must be encouraged not weakened.

TIME magazine in a 1990 article gave this advice to the boss who had a difficult office worker:

Don't argue. Instead, by being willing to make honest admissions of failure or inadequacy (if proved) you take the wind out of Awkward Joe's sails and make the possibility of good rapport likely. You don't lower your image – you actually enhance it by facing issues realistically without 'pulling rank'.

i. Maintain a vital intercessory ministry for *each* worker. *Give time* to intense systematic praying for all workers and their families. (The counter-attack of the enemy is often through the family.) Study techniques of intercession in the Scriptures (see Chapter 10 for further details).

If you discover that a worker has very little prayer support at home, do something about it.

Encourage every worker to have a 1 + 4 intercessory team. (The '4' agree to give time for definite prayer for the missionary each day. The missionary guarantees to write a letter to each of the '4' once a month.)

2. Resignations and the national church

If a worker has been working with the national church it will be wise to bring the leader into consultations surrounding a possible or actual resignation. National leaders may be able to shed light on the background to the resignation and in any case it is imperative that the church should fully realise the reasons for the mission accepting it.

On one large field there was consternation among church leaders when they discovered that the field had accepted a worker's resignation without any consultation with them. Relationships were damaged for a long time.

3. Resignations and the worker's home church

While it is a laudable motive to shield a resigning worker from enquiries as to the underlying reasons, it is unwise to keep the home church 'in the dark' – especially if that church has been supporting the worker by prayer and finance.

It is wise to inform the pastor and senior elders of an impending resignation as early as possible. If there is conflict between the resigning person and the mission, it will be unfortunate if the church hears from the worker first, because its attitude will undoubtedly be coloured by the explanations given.

See International Guidelines, 1986 Ed. (pp 39-40) for further guidance on handling resignations due to moral failure.

4. Final check

Here is a checklist of questions to ask if a worker has given an indication of resigning:

- What is the *real* cause? (It may not be the one stated.)
- If he has a grievance, is it legitimate?
- Am I part of the cause? (If so, seek an in-depth consultation, preferably in the presence of a third party.)
- Does his intended resignation stem from an inherent personal weakness?
- If so, how can I (or someone else) minister to that weakness?
- Is his faculty of judgement impaired for any cause? (Fatigue,

discouragement, marital problems, other relationships, physical problems, stress, etc.)

- Can the debilitating factor be dealt with?
- Has he failed to find a ministry, or shown inadequacy in ministry?
- Is he gifted for the ministry he has been asked to take on?
- Has anyone in the fellowship failed him? (Leader, deputy leader, committee member, nearest WEC team member.)
- Is he resigning out of negative reaction or positive leading to go to some other ministry? If it is negative reaction, how can this be addressed?

5. Ten main reasons why people have left WEC

Reason		1966-75		1976-86
a. Emotional/temperamental/ spiritual inadequacy		13.5		13.3
b. Lack of commitment to or dissatisfaction with:				
i WEC's *Ps and P*	2.9		3.6	
ii Leadership (any level)	1.9	10.7	5.7	12.9
iii Administration/policy/ programmes	5.9		3.6	
c. Inability to find, develop or maintain a ministry		8.5		9.5
d. Marriage outside of WEC		8.5		10.0
e. Moral failure		3.2		9.0
f. Charismatic issue		8.5		2.9
g. Relationship with others		6.9		3.8
h. Call to another mission		6.6		4.8
i. Uncertainty re call		--		8.1
j. Faith life/finance		6.6		1.4

While statistics of resignation since 1987 are in hand, there is no data on the reasons for them. Percentages given are percentages of the total number of resignations, *not* percentages of mission membership.

Questions for study and discussion

1. Research the incidence of resignations from your field/base/ ministry. What can be learned from this? (Any repetitive reasons? Timing of resignations? Handling by leader/committee?)

2. Is there a good flow of information from bases to you about new workers arriving? Is there a good flow of information re worker assessment reaching bases from you? Could this be improved? How?

3. What factors would make you take a lenient view of someone who wanted to leave your field/ministry, but not leave WEC?

4. What more could bases/fields/leaders/committees/Regional Secretaries (RSs)/International Office (IO) do to reduce the incidence of resignations?

Bibliography

M. Douglas, *Success can be Yours* (Grand Rapids, MI: Zondervan, 1968)

R. Foster, *Celebration of Discipline* (London, UK: Hodder & Stoughton, 1980)

H. Guinness, *Sacrifice* (London, UK: IVF 5th Ed, 1966)

F. Renich, *What Happens When You Meet You* (Wheaton, IL: Tyndale House, 1975)

C. Scott (Ed.), 'Articles on Resignation', *The WECCER*, (Gerrards Cross, Bucks: WEC Publications, Oct & Dec issues 1991)

SECTION II

RELATIONSHIPS

4

Fostering Fellowship

Richard Halverson, senior pastor of the Fourth Presbyterian Church in Washington, D.C. (which has several associate pastors), writes:

> *We give priority to persons not programs. We have an explicit commitment, first to Christ then to spouse and family, then to one another (as pastors) and to the officers and people of the church, in that order. We take our relationship seriously and practise fellowship on the basis of the formula found in Matthew 18:15-35.*
>
> We treat alienation as intolerable, seek reconciliation as soon as possible when a breach occurs, and strive to maintain a loving, caring, affirming, supportive community.
>
> *Personal relationships take precedence over the work in staff meetings as well as in official board meetings. We meet with the entire staff weekly, and always our primary concern is personal or family interests. When needs are expressed we unite in prayer and take any other action possible to respond to the need. The associates (pastors) set aside one full day monthly to be together in worship, fellowship, sharing and planning ...*

Factors that foster fellowship

1. Leadership style

As the previous quotation reveals, when the leader has fellowship as a dominant concern, fellowship is present. But we are not all Richard Halversons!

It is best to realise that we each have a naturally distinctive leadership style (some of these are listed below) but that it is possible – once aware of our own style – *to consciously supplement it with a fellowship emphasis*.

Some of the main leadership styles:

	Style	Strength	Contribution to fellowship
a. Organiser/ manager	Administrative	Efficiency increased	Tends to overlook fellowship
b. Visionary/ strategist	Prophetic	Progress, action, goal orientated	Not usually a strong feature
c. Activist/ initiator	Directive	Achievement	Not likely to contribute
d. Troubleshooter/ analyst	Diplomatic	Problems solved	Can be helpful
e. Counsellor/carer	Pastoral	Good team welfare	Very positive re fellowship
f. Training/ facilitator	Delegative	Team potential grows	Likely to be helpful
g. Consolidator/ improver	Perfectionist	Not much growth, but operation improved	Fellowship likely to increase
h. Consensus seeker	Consultative	Unity and harmony	Strong fellowship development

This list will also help us to be aware of the pitfalls attached to certain leadership styles (note carefully a., b., c.).

41

2. Personal lifestyle

As well as having a leadership style the leader will also have a personal bias either towards majoring on *work* or majoring on *people*.

	The people-orientated leader will:	The work-orientated leader will:
a.	value relationships more than achievement.	prefer to work in isolation, concentrate on the task rather than the people.
b.	see people as ends not means.	see people as means to achieving goals.
c.	be sensitive to person's needs.	be unable to sense when tensions are building up.
d.	be approachable.	be withdrawn
e.	be vulnerable – ready to admit fallibilities, needs, failures.	be defensive and rigid in decision making.

Some have found the following diagram helpful:

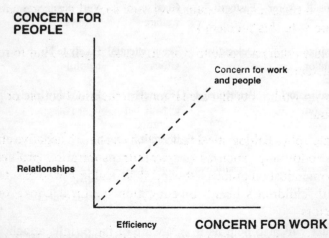

The wise leader will obviously seek to find a balance indicated by the dotted line.

3. Leader's attitude, aims, and actions

There is no doubt that the key factor in the quality of fellowship on a field/base/ministry is the aims, actions and attitudes of the leader. The corporate team-sense can be maximised or crushed, depending on the leader's sense of values in this area. How can a leader practically promote a strong team fellowship?

a. Give fellowship a high priority and minister principles of fellowship to the group (see next section).

b. Develop a pastoral concern for workers. Visit regularly; be approachable.

c. Have a warm and supportive attitude to workers and their ministries.

d. Be open and frank; this will encourage the same in the team.

e. Arrange opportunities for team fellowship on a regular basis.

f. Do not allow the work to become so spread out that fellowship meetings become too expensive. (Special conditions that exist, e.g. in trans-national teams, will need special arrangements to cope with this problem.)

g. Help workers not only to work and pray together, but to relax together.

h. Set up work units that are larger than the usual couple or pair teams.

i. Watch physical/logistical factors that can have a negative effect on fellowship, such as overwork/transportation problems/ communication problems/financial difficulties/ problems to do with children's health or education/ cultural background factors.

j. Set sensible conference schedules that allow folks to unwind and relax, as well as do business.

k. Make sure that conference times provide opportunity to enter into one anothers' concerns and problems, and to identify with each other in prayer and intercession.

l. Learn to ask the kind of questions that open up nitty-gritty areas, such as:

- What is your biggest hassle these days?
- Are you feeling fulfilled in your ministry?
- What factor encourages you most?
- What factor discourages you most?
- How do you divide your time between ministry and family?
- Are you getting through to the Lord?
- Do you feel you are moving towards your goals?

m. Make use of a yearly questionnaire covering all aspects of ministry and life in general. This generally brings out areas that need attention. Typical questions might be:

- How do you evaluate your workload?
- Have you found it easy to obtain advice and counsel?
- Do you have a sense of fulfilment or frustration for your year's work?
- How could your effectiveness be improved?
- Have you fitted in happily to the team's strategy?

'People won't care how much you know until they know how much you care.'

n. A general comment:
The writer, as a former International Secretary, can state unequivocally, that field and base leaders who major on maintaining close relationships, encouraging supportiveness and interdependence and who give a personal lead in openness and brokenness as a way of life, have teams that thrive, are effective, stay on the job, and attract new workers.

4. Awareness and implementation of the biblical requirements of fellowship

Norman Grubb's experience of the Ruanda Mission's emphasis on fellowship – coming from God's dealings with that mission along the lines of 1 John, chapters 1 and 2 – led to the adoption of the 'fellowship' pillar of WEC, but one would have to say it is an elusive pillar and the degree to which it is practised varies widely throughout the mission.

There has been a consistent pattern of new candidates thoroughly enjoying the fellowship life at HQ during candidate course, yet languishing in a field or ministry situation because it is not being practised. We have much to learn!

If we study the phrase 'one another' in the New Testament we will find a large amount of teaching regarding relationships:

a. Be devoted (Rom. 12:10)
b. Honour (Rom. 12:10)
c. Live in harmony (Rom. 12:16)
d. Love (Rom. 13:8ff)
e. Don't criticise (Rom. 14:13)
f. Counsel (Rom. 15:14)
g. By love serve (Gal. 5:13)
h. Don't provoke (Gal. 5:26)
i. Bear one another's burdens (Gal. 6:2)
j. Have the same mind, love, purpose (Phil. 2:2)
k. Be kind, tender-hearted (Eph. 4:32)
l. Submit (Eph. 5:21)
m. Don't lie (Col. 3:9)
n. Have patience (Col. 3:12)
o. Forgive, bear with (Col. 3:13)
p. Teach and counsel (Col. 3:16)
q. Stimulate to love and good works (Heb. 10:24)
r. Don't neglect to meet with (Heb. 10:25)
s. Encourage (Heb. 10:25)
t. Don't slander (Jas. 4:11)

u. Confess your faults (Jas. 5:16)
v. Give hospitality (1 Pet. 4:9)
w. Serve one another with your spiritual gifts (1 Pet. 4:10)
x. Walk in the light and have fellowship (1 John 1:7)

5. Leader's awareness of what keeps workers, and keeps them happy

Consciously or unconsciously every new worker reaches his target field/base/ministry with certain expectations. From research in the business and Christian world, here are a number of factors which he or she will wish to experience:

a.	A sense of *fulfilment*	Doing what one feels called to do – a task for which one feels equipped.
b.	A sense of *achievement*	Accomplishing a worthwhile task that is in line with accepted goals.
c.	A sense of *belonging*	Being part of a united and supportive team.
d.	A sense of *responsibility*	Knowing the extent and limits of one's task and one's authority.
e.	A sense of *acceptance*	Knowing one is wanted and valued. This comes from the expressed appreciation of the leader.
f.	A sense of *participation*	Being able to be part of the decision-making process.
g.	A sense of *direction*	Being able to identify with the team's agreed objectives and strategies.
h.	A sense of *awareness*	Having all the information needed to do the job and understand its ramifications.
i.	A sense of *opportunity for growth and development*	This comes largely from the leader's encouragement to develop further skills, but also from the outlook of the team.

j.	A sense of *understanding*	Knowing *exactly* what is required in order to be rated a *success* in the job.
k.	A sense of *being cared for*	This comes from the knowledge that the leader is personally and pastorally concerned about one's welfare.
l.	A sense of *freedom*	Being given scope to do the task without unnecessary interference.

It is the leader's task to check and ensure that these expectations are being fulfilled and to take steps to remedy situations that militate against their fulfilment.

Factors that hinder fellowship

Fellowship just does not 'happen'; it has to be created and maintained. The leader is the catalyst. Numerous factors can lead to the absence or breakdown of fellowship and some of these are listed below. (The opposite of fellowship is conflict; conflict resolution is such a large and important subject that it will be treated in a separate chapter.)

1. Dissatisfying factors

Dr Kenneth Gangel in *Competent to Lead* says:

> *Our prime deficiency (as leaders) lies ... in our failure to recognise the presence of 'dissatisfiers'. The problem develops because we have frequently failed to recognise their existence and have concentrated our attention on multiplying and enhancing the 'satisfiers' while the 'dissatisfiers' may have been chipping away at the morale – and consequently the motivation – of our workers.*

Some dissatisfiers:

a. Unhappy inter-personal relationships (with peer groups or leader/s).

47

b. Low view of leader's capability in attitudes or abilities.

c. Lack of conviction about or commitment to group goals and strategies.

d. Sub-standard conditions under which the task is being carried out (physical, climatical, social, cultural, economic).

e. Discouragement or depression due to lack of results, lack of appreciation, lack of pastoral care.

f. Weariness in the spiritual conflict, or non-awareness of it.

g. Health factors.

2. Lack of understanding of the leader/led relationship

An unspoken 'contract' has to exist between the leader and the led if a harmonious relationship is to be maintained. Each party has to 'pay' for the benefit gained from the other party; this is often not realised and difficulties arise when one side makes demands on the other without seeing the need to 'make payment' for what it hopes to receive.

What the team member expects from the leader:	What he has to pay to obtain these:
a. Appreciation, recognition	Loss of individualism – has to be part of a team, relegating some degree of personal freedom for good of group.
b. Counsel	
c. Encouragement	
d. Guidance	
e. Security	
f. Pastoral care	
g. Help	
h. Fellowship	

What the leader expects from the team member:	What he has to pay to obtain these:
a. Loyalty	Loss of 'personal' ministry.
b. Respect	Constant demand of wellbeing of team.
c. Goodwill	Intercessory ministry for team
d. Co-operation	General and pastoral care and helpfulness.
c. Task accomplishment	

Historical note

As leader of WEC in 1950 Norman Grubb was deeply troubled. In field after field there had been fellowship breakdowns. The great pioneers of faith who had opened new fields in South America, Africa and Asia were weak in fostering fellowship. He cried to the Lord for an answer – and found it, when, returning from a visit to the Zaire (Congo) field, he stayed a while at a CMS station in Uganda. He found a wonderful level of fellowship between missionaries and nationals. The secret – brokenness and openness in personal relations.

He asked the mission to send representatives to London. Two Africans came and all available personnel were called in to hear them.

God used their testimony to bring about a totally new level of fellowship in the mission. It can be truly said that these meetings were a turning point in its history.

Questions for study and discussion

1. Discuss with committee members the fellowship level existing in your team. How could it be improved?

2. Is there any dominant factor that is 'bugging' workers and keeping them from a sense of fulfilment?

3. Do the workers understand the leader/led contract? Would some explanation be helpful?

4. Has any teaching on fellowship been given lately? Is it needed?

5. Are there instances of alienation still prevalent? How should these be handled?

6. How should undercurrents of dissatisfaction be handled?

7. What can be done on your field/base to foster fellowship?

Bibliography

K. Gangel, *Competent to Lead* (Chicago, USA: Moody Press, 1974)

A. Getz, *Building Up One Another* (Wheaton, IL: Victor Books, 1980)

N. Grubb, *Continuous Revival* (London, UK: CLC, 1952)

R. Hession, *The Calvary Road* (London, UK: CLC, 1950)

M. Lee, *Leadership/Followership* (Beaverlodge, Alberta: Horizon Books, 1983)

5

Conflict

The potential for conflict varies enormously. Where a team faces intense resistance to the gospel internal fellowship is likely to be strong. Where workers are having adequate fellowship with national church folk, internal fellowship tends to be weak. Poor team relationships can also occur when units are widespread and seldom meet.

1. Causes of internal conflict

a. Leadership insensitivity

When a leader does not have a pastoral gift and fails to visit team members, those who are under pressure tend to feel neglected and can develop a negative, critical attitude which can lead to conflict. Often opposition to proposals can really be opposition to the leader rather than to the proposal itself.

b. Mutual role expectancy

Leaders can be disappointed with members' performance. Workers can be disappointed with leaders. The real cause may well be *inadequate communication*. It is imperative that every one from the leader to the newest recruit has a detailed Job Description that includes:

- a general statement of the purpose of the task
- a list of specific duties
- line of accountability
- period of operation
- mechanism for review.

Job Descriptions should be a matter of discussion and negotiation, and should never be imposed arbitrarily. Every person should know what is expected, and the extent of responsibility carried.

c. Ministry possessiveness

Workers can become too attached to their job and defensive about change. Often their job becomes their security. Also, when sub-teams or ministries exist within a field or base it is very easy for the members to become so absorbed in their task that they cease to be concerned for the larger group, or for their region, or the organisation in general. Any discussion regarding future development can be seen only in terms of how it will affect their own sub-group.

d. Doctrinal mistrust

Generally, we have reached a reasonable level of tolerance but there is still some degree of mistrust, especially between charismatics and non-charismatics. Both sides have weaknesses. The charismatics tend to exert pressure for others to have a similar experience; the non-charismatics feel that the others are experience-oriented and lack theological depth. In most cases, convictions have more to do with personal background than strict theological reasoning or Biblical interpretation.

e. Generation gap

Over the past 10-15 years vast changes have occurred in the societies from which most recruits have come. Every field and base with a mixture of older and younger generations of workers needs to list this subject for special study. See Chapter 9.

f. Lack or loss of confidence in a leader

This can happen when a leader

- lacks organisational skills, leading to inequality of work-loads, low morale, etc.

- breaks confidence.

- breaks a promise.

- fails to grasp the reasons for a worker's viewpoint.

- appears insensitive to a worker's problem.

- fails to express appreciation.

- fails to give encouragement, particularly in a time of stress.

- adopts an autocratic attitude.

- is more work oriented than person oriented.

- fails to implement decisions made in the fellowship.

- reveals a lack of ability to minister to the spiritual needs of the body.

g. Low self-image

This is an insidious and prevalent condition that affects many workers. Because they lack confidence they 'wear masks', seldom share their views publicly, and grumble a lot in private. They tend to be defensive of their own views and compensate for their own perceived limitations by being critical of others. Leaders need to bend over backwards in drawing out their views in conferences. Otherwise undercurrents and conflict will mar the workings of the team.

h. Stress

Often the true cause of conflict is not the apparent triggering circumstances but an underlying stress factor or medical factor in an individual, causing low tolerance of tensions, difficulties or problems. The worker under stress needs careful and consistent pastoral care. See Chapter 13 on Stress.

i. Short-cut decision making

A team can move too quickly into decision making on import-ant policy and strategy matters without waiting on God or praying through to the kind of consensus that Colossians 3:15 mentions. This hurried procedure can lead to conflict later as differences of opinion are expressed.

j. Newcomers opposing current strategies

All new arrivals need to have explained to them the obligation to accept and flow with strategies that are already in place. The time to express reservations should really be at the next arranged time of review.

k. New worker resentment of leader's periodic assessments
Two things can be done to prevent this:

• Try to have a broad-based assessment by seeking opinions of committee members or senior workers.

• *Always* have reasons and instances to prove any points of criticism that are shared. Avoid generalities, e.g. 'We don't think you have a good attitude about...' Never file or mail an assessment without the worker being given a chance to comment.

l. The prospect of change in ministry pattern, policies or even location can lead to conflict. (See Chapter 9 on Change, and note the instructions on how to prepare workers for change.)

m. **Excluding workers from participation** in discussions that affect him or his ministry will cause conflict. If the worker is on home leave await his return before finalising a decision.

2. Resolving conflict – general underlying principles

a. **Fellowship just does not happen automatically**
The leader has to work to create it and work to preserve it. He is the key to success.

b. **Good communication is another key**
By keeping the lines of communication open between yourself and team members you will help to create an 'early warning system' for detecting potential conflict. Are you sharing all the information you can?

c. **Use a prayer list that includes every member of your team**
Remember a leader is meant to be an intercessor. See Hebrews 13:17, 1 Samuel 12:23. An intercessory ministry releases the power of God into your team members' lives, and also heightens your sensitivity to their needs.

d. **Major on prayer in every team activity**
The team that prays together stays together. Encourage prayer retreats. Lead team prayer times by giving adequate information and guidance in the actual praying and train others to lead. Preach on prayer. Model prayer. Help members to see that strong faith is the result of prayer. Prayer is the battleground; service is picking up the spoils. Discuss spiritual warfare. Seek a strategy on prayer and prayer goals. Bring the team together regularly for prayer even though it costs money.

e. Model servant leadership

Good servants always have uppermost in their minds the *needs* of those they are serving. Anticipate needs; meet needs; or show how needs can be met. Servant leaders do not make enemies, they win friends.

f. Teach and model the principle of the Cross and the principle of walking in the light.

As with physical procreation so with spiritual procreation. We reproduce what we are and what we teach. If we have fully embraced the principle of the Cross people will sense our brokenness and utter dependence on God, they will sense our total sufficiency in the resurrection life of Jesus and they will realise we are men of prayer, living at the throne. As Oswald Sanders once said, 'Disciples beget disciples.'

g. Think sideways

Before taking any course of action pause to ask yourself: Who will be affected by this? Have I considered their reaction? Have I consulted sufficiently? Is there a less painful way of doing it? Who else needs to know?

h. If initiating change:

Fully explain the need of change, and give plenty of time for people to adjust to the idea. Listen to objections and check whether opposition revolves round the idea or around *you*. (See Chapter 9 on Change.)

i. Make maximum use of the field committee as a means of avoiding conflict

Use as a sounding board for ideas. Seek members' help in picking up the field's reactions to proposals. Invite committee members' co-operation in formulating policy and strategy. Delegate research to them if more information is needed. Go over potentially 'dangerous' agenda items with them before staff conferences. (But avoid giving the impression that everything is 'sewn up'.)

3. Points to remember in the conflict resolution process

a. Strenuously avoid a 'winner/loser' outcome. Usually both points of view have some merit. Aim for a *win/win* outcome, and strive for a full understanding of the other party's position.

b. Work towards identifying the broad areas of agreement and move towards identifying the area of disagreement. This then becomes the area of negotiation.

c. Tackle the *problem* not the *people*!

d. Let each party in the dispute accurately describe the problem as it affects them. 'Once we know we have been heard, we are usually ready to move on to compromise.' (Dayton and Engstrom)

e. Ensure that each party can tackle issues without emotion. If not possible, delay until they can.

f. Be ethical and be fair.

g. Be objective, and use language that shows it.

h. If the issue revolves round policy or strategy it may be advantageous to have small groups analyse it and report back to the total group.

i. Is some important factor being overlooked in:

- the historical background?
- thc person's home country background?
- the culture?
- the mission's principles, manuals, guidelines?

And is your own personal attitude right?

j. Don't argue using generalisations. (Avoid *always* and *never*.)

k. Don't use ultimatums or threats, real or implied.

l. Don't belittle another's status/intelligence/reasoning.

m. Don't take advantage of your status/seniority/experience.

n. Don't use history/tradition/the status quo/cultural – as distinct from Biblical – norms, to justify your position.

4. Final check

Here are some check questions to be asked before a conclusion is reached:

a. Has each party's needs been met?

b. Has any prejudice, emotion, tradition, party-spirit or strong personality predominated?

c. Has all information needed been available?

d. Have decisions been made out of stress/tiredness/lack of time/ desperation?

e. If relevant, was the Biblical procedure in Matthew 18:15-17 followed? (Step 1 – Show the fault to the offending brother. Step 2 – If no response, take one or two others. Step 3 – If still unresponsive, involve the church.)

f. Was the Biblical principle of 'preferring one another' present?
(Phil. 2:3-4; Eph. 5:21; Col. 3:12; Rom. 10:12; 1 Pet. 5:5.)

g. Is someone who is going to be seriously affected by the decision being left out of the decision?

5. Examples of conflict resolution

a. On large field 'X' there was conflict between a sub-team working at a distance from the main centre and the rest of the team. It was resolved by the leader promising to increase his visits to the distant area and by the sub-team promising not to take unilateral action on policy matters.

b. In a geographically small field 'Y' a member resigned and commenced an independent mission. This action was seen by the field as complicating the situation before the government.

In the resolution process the team apologised for its arbitrary handling of the ex-member. He, in turn, agreed to confine the new mission's activities to areas where WEC was not working. Relations are now good.

c. While there has been much blessing on field 'Z' a serious split arose between two factions, each headed by a strong personality and each having a different view regarding spiritual gifts. The field divided, but with encouragement to retain and rebuild good personal relationships the issue has been resolved and a good working relationship re-established.

Questions for study and discussion

1. State in short sentences the principles of conflict resolution taught in Matthew 18:15-22; Colossians 3:12-15; and 1 John 1:5-10, 2:9-11.

2. Evaluate the outcome of the Jerusalem conference in Acts 15 from the point of view of the instructions given in this chapter.

3. In your situation are there causes of conflict not listed in Section I? What would be the right course of action in dealing with them?

Bibliography

S. Dinnen, *Here We Stand* (Gerrards Cross, Bucks, UK: WEC Publications)

N. Grubb, *Continuous Revival* (London, UK: CLC, 1952)

T. Wierda, *Relationships* (Gerrards Cross, UK: WEC Publications, 1989)

D. Palmer, *Managing Conflict Creatively* (Pasadena, USA: William Carey Library, 1990)

6

Facilitating

1. Adding or multiplying?

Missionary Bob sets out to plant a church and succeeds, even though it happens slowly. Because none of his people have training or experience he does most of the preaching and teaching. His people generously affirm him in his ministry. He has invested fifteen years in this work and does not want to hand over too early, before his folk are mature ... He feels this may take some years ...

Safe, slow, sensible; high spiritual standards.

But meet Geoff, working in the same culture. He *facilitates* the starting of churches. He motivates and trains people to do it. He is not up front every Sunday. He encourages new Christians and develops leaders right from the start. He will not start church services unless he has nationals to lead them. Geoff's ministry keeps expanding as he trains leaders to take over. He has been in the same city as Bob but only for four years. He has seen two churches established and is working towards a third. The total membership is much bigger than Bob's group. (Source: Glenn Kendall, *Evangelical Missions Quarterly*, July '88)

Of course, many questions arise. How do we evaluate 'maturity'? How do we know when nationals can handle leadership humbly and effectively? Is it not dangerous to have them 'up front' so much?

a. Career missionary – a misnomer

And yet ... and yet ... Even though there are strong reasons for hastening slowly, could it be true that we can easily fall into the trap that awaits the 'career missionary' – namely making a 'career' for himself? The truth is that on some WEC fields there is no timetable for handing over! Paul did not stay on endlessly in one location. He operated as a facilitator.

b. True leadership
The essential nature of leadership has to do, not with *satisfaction* through *personal achievement* but with *fulfilment* through *others' development*. It is investment in other lives that counts. In many of our fields where we have national churches the only justification for our continued presence is that we train potential leaders. Why should we pastor churches when we can be training pastors? D. L. Moody said, 'I would rather put 1,000 men to work than do the work of 1,000 men.'

c. Responsibility is the key to personal growth
The key to development and growth is having to carry responsibility. Responsibility makes or breaks, but for the growing Christian it usually 'makes'. So we need a mind-set that is *constantly seeking ways of transferring responsibility to others*. When Andrew Carnegie was asked what was the secret of his success he said, 'It is very simple; I am merely a man who knows how to enlist men better than myself.'

2. What are the steps in good facilitating?

a. Cultivate
Seek to recognise workers' gifts and encourage them to have an effective ministry where they are. Create an environment where *failure* is not *fatal*, but nevertheless aim for high standards of excellence.

b. Motivate
Give them goals in personal growth development and ministry. Encourage them to take courses that will improve their skills.

c. Initiate

Have areas of responsibility thought out for those to whom you plan to delegate later. Be able to define the task and the objectives.

d. Delegate

Actually transfer responsibility and give sufficient authority for the person to carry out the tasks allotted. (But remember you are still finally responsible – so there is a risk!) Delegate to the person who has the potential to develop.

Delegation is a process whereby higher authority exchanges a given weight of authority and responsibility for an equal weight of obligation and accountability. (Peter Wiwcharuk)

e. Educate

Give all the instruction and information necessary for the delegate to carry out his task successfully. Training should be a major part of our strategy.

f. Liberate

Don't breathe down the delegate's neck. Give freedom to act and make decisions. If you don't give scope for initiative you are not delegating, but directing.

g. Invigilate

Stay close! Be discreetly watchful and available for giving advice and help. In the final extremity, stand by to rescue!

h. Congratulate

Give the delegate credit and recognition for what he/she has achieved.

3. Hindrances to good facilitating

a. Unconscious or even conscious desire to do everything oneself.

b. Workaholism. Being so task-conscious that we lose sight of people as our real goal.

c. Conviction that no one can do the job as well as yourself.

d. Insecurity. (The existence and structure of your present task creates a sense of security for you.)

e. Lack of trust in others.

f. Fear of stress related to correcting others' mistakes.

g. Lack of vision for the development of others.

h. Over-critical attitude towards others and their performance.

i. Perfectionism. Demand for unrealistic standards in others.

j. Failure to realise that people grow faster when they are carrying responsibility.

k. Fear of supporters' reactions if you are not seen to be an achiever.

l. Lack of faith in the Holy Spirit in other people.

m. Dislike of change.

n. Prejudice (only certain people can do certain tasks).

4. Facilitating in the context of church planting/ nurture

a. *We can't build indigenous churches*

The following are some quotations from a perceptive article by J. Michael Kuiper in *Evangelical Missions Quarterly* of October 1988:

It is a simple contradiction to speak of a missionary working to build an indigenous church. As long as he *builds it, it is not indigenous. Failure to step aside leads to dependency. By-products of this are inferiority and resentment which reinforce passivity, cripple initiative and prevent new adventures in faith.*

b. *Olson's Venezuelan experience*

Kuiper draws attention to some of the methods used by Bruce Olson among the Motilone Indians of Venezuela:

> *Olson never offered any format for worship or advice on Christian ethics ... When on occasion a Motilone asked his advice he told them to ask the elders.*
>
> *Education was accepted because Olson refused to teach children even though they were eager and fast learners. Rather he taught the old men. In this way he did not disrupt the leadership or threaten the elders' position of wisdom and status. After the elders had learned a bit and identified with the process they endorsed and promoted the educational system.*
>
> *Olson established no institutions that were dependent on him or any outside worker for maintenance.*
>
> *One time half the tribe became desperately ill. Olson had the appropriate medicine, but rather than distribute it he tried to persuade the witch-doctor to use it, but without success. Olson deliberately contracted the disease himself and then asked the witch-doctor to give him the medicine. When he got well he gave his gratitude to the witch-doctor who now eagerly dispensed the cure to others. Since then medical stations have been set up throughout hundreds of miles of Motilone territory.*

5. Are we serious?

If we are really serious about facilitating rather than achieving we will be:

a. making training at all levels our main strategy and activity.

b. involving nationals at every level of outreach.

c. involving nationals in every aspect of worship services and meetings.

d. carefully seeking to discern their spiritual gifts and ensuring there is scope for their use (1 Pet. 4:10; 1 Cor. 12:7; Rom. 12:4-6).

e. wisely matching areas of service with spiritual gifts.

f. establishing an agreed timetable for shedding the responsibilities we presently carry.

g. strenuously resisting pressure to do what nationals can do or be trained to do.

Note the instruction that God gave to Moses regarding the one to whom he was delegating leadership: *'Commission* Joshua and *encourage* and *strengthen* him ...'* (Deut. 3:28).

Historical note

As far as development of WEC in the early days is concerned, undoubtedly the most significant event was C. T. Studd's delegating of mission leadership at home to Norman Grubb. While Studd continued in Congo, Grubb had unbridled freedom to develop the work as God led him in the homeland.

In actual fact Grubb was far more successful in keeping men and women loyal to the mission than Studd was.

But it was Studd's genius in delegating to Grubb that led to the fast development of a WEC work force in Britain and in the start of numerous new fields.

Grubb in turn learned to facilitate others and to entrust big leadership responsibilities to them.

Questions for study and discussion

1. What tasks are you doing that could be done by others?
2. How can we make the transfer from being a *doer* to being an *enabler*? What factors are involved?
3. Can the principles of this chapter be applied equally well to national workers as to fellow missionaries? Are there additional factors that need to be kept in mind?
4. For you personally what pitfalls exist in delegating to others?
5. What factors in another worker would create sufficient confidence for you to transfer responsibility to him/her?

Bibliography

L. Eims, *Be a Motivational Leader* (Wheaton, IL: Victor Books, 1981)

A.L. McGinnis, *Bringing Out the Best in People* (Minneapolis, MI: Augsburg, 1985)

7

The Leadership Concept in WEC

1. History

The leadership concept in WEC has gone through a number of changes since the mission began. In the early days – the twenties, thirties and forties – when we were almost entirely engaged in pioneering new fields there was an emphasis on strong, indeed autocratic, leadership. We had tough, indomitable men of faith who pushed through with their tasks with determination and thrust. Strong leadership was needed and it was given. Leaders at that time had continuous appointment.

But with the build-up of teams, crises of fellowship arose in many of our fields; the pioneers were not necessarily good pastoral carers. So changes had to be made. No longer was the initial pioneer the automatic leader. Elections were instituted in which the rank-and-file members chose a leader every three years. The emphasis shifted to fellowship and this, though much safer, led to a slowing down of the work. Every major (and even minor) decision had to be ratified by the fellowship. The leader became a consensus-gatherer and chairman of the field committee. The fifties, sixties and seventies were our 'fellowship' phase.

In the later seventies and eighties the pendulum swung back to the middle and we came into a healthier phase in which there was a desire for leaders to lead, to have and take initiative, to bring out proposals for development and advance, and at the same time, a desire for the fellowship to exercise its role as assessor, balancing and checking any wrong or misguided proposals or initiatives.

2. The situation today

Three-year elections continue; all fields have to have a deputy leader, nominated by the leader but appointed by the fellowship. And field committees work with these two in the running of field affairs.

Every leader should have a job description that has been evolved by the field or field committee. The whole team and prospective leaders should consult this before an appointment is finalised.

3. The Field Committee

The members of this committee are also elected every three years. Its main tasks are to:

a. advise the leader.

b. act as a sounding board for the leader's ideas.

c. act as representatives of the members of the field.

d. discuss major field conference matters beforehand, with a view to bringing recommendations to the conference.

e. assist the leader in the evaluation of new workers.

f. handle any personnel problems in fellowship with the leader.

4. Accountability

Accountability permeates all levels of WEC administration. No one can 'go it alone'. Thus:

a. The International Secretary is accountable to the Coordinating Council and Leaders' Council.

b. Regional Secretaries are accountable to the International Secretary and the Coordinating Council.

c. Field and base leaders are accountable to the annual field conference of workers.

5. Main responsibilities of leaders

    a. Initiation and implementation of objectives and strategy. (Approval lies with conference.)
    b. Pastoral care of all workers.
    c. Orientation, language-learning arrangements, and the assessment and placement of new workers.
    d. Development of workers' gifts and ministries.
    e. Maintenance of unity and cultivation of a fellowship spirit.
    f. Full co-operation with his committee.
    g. Church/mission liaison and training of national leaders.
    h. Transfer of responsibility from mission to church.
    i. Communications within field and between field and bases/ Regional Secretaries/International Office.

6. The balance in leader-led relationships

What is the right balance between the authority of the leader and the authority of the group? It is obvious from 1 Peter 5:3 that a domineering autocratic form of leadership is not the scriptural pattern. Actually, the opposite is taught. The teaching of Christ in Matthew 20:26-28 makes it clear that the leader must be pre-eminently a *servant*. His particular *service* to the group is that he leads it. (See Chapter 1.)

It seems scriptural from the situation described in Acts 6:1-6 that the total fellowship carries ultimate authority, but a large group by its nature is incapable of initiative-taking, policy-forming, or crisis-handling. This has to be carried by the leader or a small leadership group. The fellowship comes into its own in evaluating, approving, questioning, rejecting or postponing.

7. Authority

In the final analysis what is the basis of a leader's authority? We suggest it ultimately stems from five sources:

a. The authority of God's anointing. (*Entrusted* by the Lord.)
b. The authority of his acquired knowledge. (His *expertise*.)
c. The authority of his maturity in the work. (His *experience*.)
d. The authority gained from fellow workers' respect for the quality of his life and work. (*Earned respect*.)
e. The authority of his appointment. (His *election* – the 'legal' basis.)

Historical note

To those of us who had the privilege of working closely with him it was obvious that our greatly beloved first International Secretary, Norman Grubb, was not a gifted administrator or pastor yet his authority in the mission was (to the best of the writer's knowledge) *never* seriously questioned. Why was this so?

Firstly, no one who had witnessed his handling of staff discussions, analysis of problems, and his capacity for discerning the leading of the Spirit in strategy situations, could ever doubt the anointing of wisdom and vision and energy he possessed. No one who lived close to him doubted that they were working with a man of God, and, of course, his early life on the field with C. T. Studd gave a rich experience. Above all else, his spiritual maturity, discernible in his dealings, ministry and writings, placed him head and shoulders above us all.

8. Role-expectancy

What does the leader expect from team members? Usually this can be answered in terms of work/activity/ministry/furtherance of agreed team objectives.

What does the team member expect from the leader? The answer is *care* and *concern*.

The leader looks for *results*; the follower looks for *recognition* based on a caring attitude on the leader's part. See Chapter 4 for further details.

9. Initiative

A good leader must take the initiative. It is his responsibility to present proposals for the development of the work. (This should be the outcome of his being a 'visionary'.) Norman Grubb in his account of the development of the leadership concept in WEC wrote:

> *The leadership, in general, was leadership-in-fellowship. I never believed a leader should be a mere chairman. No, he is God's appointed leader, which should mean that he is out-front of his co-workers in new ideas, in proposing solutions, et cetera. I never believed in the common idea of a commitee chairman keeping silent and just finally heading things up. No, he is a vital foremost member of the staff in their consultations and should therefore participate, giving his convinced views, differing where necessary, as much as any other member. However, a staff does not function by votes, which divide, but by talking together until there is a sense of unity about the Lord's mind.*

10. Field Autonomy

Ps and P state that the final authority in all matters relating to the field, its ministry and its personnel is the *field conference*.

However, there has been a growing recognition over the years that with our increasing size, complexity of ministries and volatile political situations no field is an 'island'. The following are ways in which field operations are affected by factors outside its borders:

a. The recruitment and training of new workers at sending bases.
b. The orientation and sending out of new workers.
c. Channelling of finance from bases to fields.
d. Promotion of fields and field projects at the sending base.
e. Designation of undesignated gifts by sending base finance committees for field support and projects.
f. Arranging of international conferences and seminars by the International Office in consultation with the Co-ordinating Council.
g. Arranging of regional conferences and seminars by the Regional Secretaries and the fields in the region.
h. Consultation with, and provision of specialist personnel for short or longer field assignments.
i. Special commissions and research, reports of which are made available to all (e.g. Ecclesiology Commission).

In view of the above, the terms 'autonomy' and 'independence' do not reflect the measure of interdependence and co-operation that actually exists in the mission.

11. Regional Secretaries

A great advance within our leadership structure took place in 1974 with the appointment of 'Regional Advisors' (later changed to 'Secretaries').

Sufficient to say that this move with its full development in the late seventies and in the eighties, has had a profound and advantageous effect in the whole mission.

Regional Secretaries have been able to visit fields and give advice in problem situations. They have arranged regional conferences. They have developed a spirit of concern between the fields in their areas. They have given advice on the development of new fields and ministries. They have been a tower of strength to new leaders feeling their way in a daunting task. They have provided leaders with information resource material and know-how in many areas. And their reports of field visits have been invaluable for sending base leaders, other Regional Secretaries and the personnel of the International Office.

In 1984 Patrick Johnstone said, 'The full launching of the regional structure is the most fundamental stimulus to our forward move.'

Questions for study and discussion

1. In your opinion is there a good balance in relationships between leader and led, in your field/base/ministry?
2. 'Leaders should *lead*' has been a notable cry. How far can you take this?
3. What is the basis of a leader's authority?

Bibliography

S. Dinnen (Ed), *Leader's Manual* (St Leonards, Tasmania: Resources Office of WEC International, 1980)

N. Grubb, *Once Caught, No Escape* (Autobiography) (London, UK: Lutterworth, 1969)

J. Walker (Ed), *Fool and Fanatic* (Gerrards Cross, Bucks: WEC International, 1982)

SECTION III

STRATEGY

8

Vision, Goals and Strategy

1. Lessons from WEC history

A dip into WEC history will reveal that the periods when clearcut goals were before us have been the periods of maximum growth.

It started with Norman Grubb's concern to have a worthy anniversary memorial to C.T. Studd's passing. God gave him a vision for ten new workers and the finance for their outgoing by a fixed date. The ten came in. The process repeated itself year by year with steadily increasing targets – 15, 25, 50, 75 – so WEC grew at an astonishing rate.

When, through the work of our research men, Leslie Brierley and Patrick Johnstone, fresh targets for new fields and new advances have been presented and accepted outstanding growth resulted.

2. Think it up or pray it down?

How do we approach this matter? Are goals to be arrived at by a process of logic leading from awareness of a situation to the adoption of rational objectives? Or are they to be received 'from above' as God-inspired and communicated?

Perhaps Grubb's own words may be of help. He says in *Touching the Invisible*, p.23:

We recognise and utilise the mind in its rightful position. At this point there is most confusion in the matter of guidance. Some put too much emphasis on human reason, 'common sense', confusing it with the Lord's voice: others put too little, turning from it as a

76

carnal thing and attempting to find guidance with an emptied mind. The truth is that the human reason is a pre-eminently useful servant, but was never created to be the final arbiter of truth in the human personality. Reason is the great sorting house, but not the sorter. Its function is to investigate, tabulate, theorise, but not direct. That is the function of the Spirit.

In the situations mentioned in Acts 13:1-4 (the commission to the Antioch church), Acts 16:6-10 (the vision of Macedonia) and Acts 18:9-10 (the direction to stay on in Corinth) Paul is seen to be very much a man sensitively aware of Spirit-given vision.

This is the hallmark of the spiritual leader and it is the unique feature which distinguishes him from being merely a manager.

THE LEADER	THE MANAGER
a. Motivated by vision.	Organises existing resources.
b. Knows where the team should be going.	Knows what the team should be doing.
c. Deals in concepts, ideas.	Deals with function.
d. Is concerned about opportunity, strategy.	Is concerned with efficiency and economy.
e. Is concerned with ultimate success, effectiveness.	Is concerned about immediate productivity.
f. Develops team potential.	Uses team's abilities.

3. Fail to plan and you're planning to fail!

The first three of the following points are adapted from some excellent material by Ted Engstrom in his book, *The Making of a Christian Leader*, pp 143-144:

a. Recognise *envisioning* and *goal-seeking* as the most important activities of a leader.

b. Recognise, too, that although they are all-important, they are seldom urgent.

c. Set aside specific private times for vision-getting and planning.

d. Expect God to reveal to you, and to your group, not only a general vision but specific goals that will lead to its accomplishment.

e. Establish a supportive, creative climate in committee and staff discussions.

f. Utilise other visionaries, planners and strategic thinkers in evolving, developing and clarifying proposals which can be placed before the team.

g. Teach and exemplify tolerance. Things seldom work out exactly as planned.

C.T. Studd was given a vision of the unevangelised world while he was in his cabin sailing to Africa. He did not fully understand it, but he accepted it implicitly from the Lord, in spite of all the impossibilities that stood in the way.

The optimist sees the doughnut, the pessimist sees the hole in the doughnut.

The lesson of chapter 16 of Acts is simple:

- Expect *vision*   v.9
- Be prepared to *venture*   v.10
- Trust for *victory*   vv. 13-15, 16-19, 25-32.

4. Points to ponder regarding vision and its accomplishment

a. Achievement is possible only when leader and led share a commonly held vision.

b. In a voluntary organisation vision cannot be imposed.

c. Sudden vision is not likely to be quickly accepted. Drip-feed it.

d. Members will be motivated when they have been part of the decision-making process.

78

e. Vision can grow dim. Leaders need to take steps to keep it fresh.
f. Team discussions and conferences tend to revolve around problems and practices. Always set apart time for strategy discussions.
g. When the urgent tyrannises the strategic languishes.
h. Present difficulties can blind us to future opportunities.
i. Overwork and prayerlessness erode vision and momentum.
j. The implementation of vision requires gifts different from possessing and imparting vision. If the latter are absent, ensure the visionary leader has a functionary alongside him.

5. Basic responsibilities

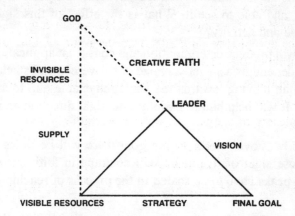

The triangle drawn with the solid lines gives the basic leadership responsibilities in terms of goals and strategy.

The leader must possess a vision of what the team's goal should be. He also needs to be intimately aware of the team's strengths and resources – its personnel and their expertise and gifting; material resources such as property, equipment, transport; its non-material assets such as experience, standing, contacts with others who can help both inside and outside of the mission. Strategy is the methods and policies that will lead to the accomplishment of sub-goals that in turn reach the ultimate goal.

The dotted line triangle shows the steps that leader and team need to take if the resources are presently not available. These amount to the exercise of strategic or creative or co-operative faith in the Lord for His provision of resources. Jesus was constantly on the lookout for such faith and when He saw it would remark on it. 'Your faith has healed you' (Luke 18:42; 8:48). 'According to your faith will it be done to you' (Matt. 9:29).

6. What the perception of clear goals does for the individual team member

Imagine the mountaineer at a distance from the peak he wishes to reach, and able to see it. What is the effect of this sight on his attitude and activity?

It will produce determination and consistent application. It will engender enthusiasm and a capacity to overcome obstacles. It will keep him moving towards the peak and enable him to avoid tangents. It will help him to maintain the right direction and to make progress.

As he moves closer to his goal there will be times when he will lose sight of it, but he will continue in faith knowing that lesser peaks have to be scaled in the process of reaching the ultimate.

When the going is rough and demanding he has the will to persevere because he has the goal clearly in his mind.

As he ascends he is able to look back or look down and see the progress he has made, comparing where he was with where he is now. Success is reaching the top and this gives the assurance that he has done all the right things.

If he has to turn back, he can, on the way, evaluate the reasons for his failure and learn valuable lessons for the next expedition.

In summary, perceiving the goal produces:

- commitment   • ability to assess progress
- determination   • strength to refuse tangents
- sense of direction • power to overcome obstacles
- continuity   • willingness for hard times
- enthusiasm   • faith

7. What having goals does for the team

Imagine the same activity undertaken by a team. What is involved?

Discussion on which peak to climb leading to unity of purpose. Commitment to support one another. Co-ordination of resources – each taking one's share of equipment and supplies. Then as the expedition proceeds – mutual encouragement and concern for one another. Increase of morale as progress is achieved. Willingness to 'give the extra' for the sake of the others. Cameraderie in facing common hardships.

In summary, mutual goal-setting in a team produces:

- unity – team spirit   • mutual encouragement
- supportiveness   • morale building
- co-ordination   • responsibility for one another
- enthusiasm   • wise use of resources

8. The three essentials of good goal-setting

A goal must have these qualities if it is going to have the desired effect of motivating a group towards its accomplishment; it must be:

a. measurable   It must be specific, clear, definable and capable of being measured against some scale.

b. sensible   It should not be too high, lest it discourage. It should not be too low, lest it does not challenge.

c. acceptable   All who are to be involved in its accomplish
                   ment should have a say in the decision-mak-
                   ing process.

9. What factors determine the strategy?

a. Time   How urgent is it? When is the most
                   propitious time?
b. Personnel   Who is to be involved? Do they have
                   the gifts?
c. Resources   Money? Equipment? Housing?
                   Transport? Contacts?
d. Needs/trends   Will we be meeting a felt need? A
                   future need?
e. Opportunity   Are the circumstances propitious?
                   Pointing in the same direction?
f. Culture   Is it in line? Will it offend? How to
                   contextualise?
g. Socio-political Is it relevant to the current social order
                   and situation?
h. Technology   Do the facilities exist to make it possible?
i. Education   Will it be understood, appreciated?
j. Communications Is it feasible, practical?

10. An example of strategy from Brazil

A Christian banker in Brazil longed to be able to reach the crowds
in his home city of three million. He cried to the Lord for a strategy. The answer was: 'Advertise your telephone number in the
newspaper and offer a free Christian counselling service.'

After the advert appeared his phone never stopped ringing!
He gave people counsel but he also invited them to attend 'lec-
tures' in a public hall. Hundreds were won to Christ and a large
church grew. WECers joined to give help, and after noting the
success of the strategy repeated the process in Montes Claros.

This led eventually to the start of the Missionary Training College there.

The strategy was *relevant*. Brazilians love to talk, to share their problems; they are gregarious. Also the phone is not threatening; if they don't like what they hear they can hang up.

Questions for study and discussion

1. Where should goals come from?
2. Need the leader be the visionary of the team?
3. Does the adoption of goals lead to bondage?
4. What are the factors in your field/base/ministry that should determine strategy?
5. In team conferences, problem solving and matters of administration often crowd out unhurried discussion on goals and strategy. What can be done about this?

Bibliography

J. Alexander, *Managing Our Work* (Downers Grove, IL: IVCF, 1975 (REV))

S. Dinnen, *After C.T Studd (condensed book)* (Fort Washington, PA: WEC International, 1990)

N. Grubb, *Touching the Invisible* (Fort Washington, PA: CLC (first published by Lutterworth, 1940), 1987)

W. Reddin, *Effective Management by Objective* (New York, USA: McGraw-Hill, 1971)

R. Schuller, *The Peak-to-Peek Principle* (New York, USA: Bantam Books, 1980)

9

The Challenge of Change

1. Change – a catalyst for fortitude or fear

Leaders need to realise that impending change can produce amazingly different reactions in people. We have the 'goers', the adventurers, the innovators who positively relish the excitement of change. At the other extreme we have the conservative traditionialists for whom change can only be seen as an unwelcome threat to their security.

The following summary may be somewhat over-simplified but it has a lot of truth in it. It will serve as a warning to leaders regarding the extreme care and caution that must be exercised when change is contemplated.

The reactions to impending change in goals, methods, procedure, strategy, policy, guidelines, location, activities or ministry can:

FOR THE ADVENTURESOME	FOR THE CONSERVATIVE
a. Be exciting.	Be threatening.
b. Be challenging.	Be daunting.
c. Be stretching.	Be disturbing.
d. Bring prospect of new experiences.	Stimulate fear of the unknown.
e. Bring possibility of improvement in morale.	Bring possibility of disaster.
f. Bring likelihood of greater effectiveness.	Bring likelihood of uncertainty and confusion.

g. Be a chance to develop new skills.	Be a means of revealing an inability to cope.
h. Stimulate faith.	Stimulate fear.
i. Be seen as a learning process.	Precipitate insecurity.
j. Be a possibility for proving God in a new context.	Create a situation of being out of one's depth.

2. Take pains to promote the pains in the neck

Leaders need to foster and encourage the 'stirrers', the analysts, the enquirers, the initiators, and the visionaries in the team. They will have the talents for spotting the need for change and may also have the capacity to introduce and manage change. They may not be the most 'comfortable' people to live with, but their value to the leader will be inestimable. Thomas Watson, a former chief executive officer of IBM, wrote the following (albeit in a secular context, but the inference is the same):

> *My most important contribution to IBM was my ability to pick strong and intelligent men and then hold them together by persuasion, by apologies, by financial incentives, by speeches, by chatting with their wives, by thoughtfulness when they were sick or involved in accidents ...*
>
> *I never hesitated to promote someone I didn't like. The comfortable assistant, the nice guy you like to go on fishing trips with, is a great pitfall. Instead, I looked for those sharp, scratchy, harsh, almost unpleasant guys who see and tell you about things as they really are. If you can get enough of them around you and have patience enough to hear them out, there is no limit to where you can go.*

The capacity for adaptation is crucial. Charles Krauthammer in a recent *TIME* essay wrote: *The West's capacity for adaptation is the key to its success*.

Samuel Huntington of Harvard says:

The real cause for the decline of nations ... is ... the phenomena of creeping inflexibility ... industrial sclerosis ... the loss of ability to change and adapt.

Mancur Olson writes in *The Rise and Decline of Nations*:

Mature societies start to decline when layers of special interest groups – inefficient producers, inflexible unions, government bureaucracies – succeed in impeding ... change.

3. Different generations – different reverberations

Reaction to impending change will also be effected by background, experience and age. The leader will do well to understand the characteristics of a generation which is later than his own!

While it is impossible to describe the characteristics of every WEC generation (pre-WWII, post-WWII, 'baby-boomers', post-1969) here is a list that tries to give a general contrast between "early WECers" and 'later WECers'.

OLDER MISSIONARIES	YOUNGER MISSIONARIES
a. Trained to memorise and repeat.	Trained to ask questions and evaluate.
b. Happy to accept the status quo.	Trained to analyse and formulate own goals.
c. Push through alone and don't expect help from others.	Expect help from team and from home churches/groups/individuals.
d. Exercise personal faith and 'crash on regardless'.	Like to share concerns/needs with those whom they think would like to know.
e. Make do with limited resources / facilities / sub-standard conditions.	Have grown up in comparative affluence; find it hard to accept tough conditions/shortages.

86

f. Are used to continuous work in reasonably secure conditions.	Have lived in unstable conditions and realise need for flexibility.
g. Usually do not seek pastoral help or counsel.	Welcome pastoral help and counsel.
h. See the need for overall direction and team management.	Prefer freedom from authority.
i. Do not easily share resources.	More readily share resources.
j. Find the younger generation self-centred.	Find older generation work-centred.
k. Put work first, well ahead of family needs.	Give high priority to family needs and relationships.

4. What attitudes are needed in the leader who is going to cope with change?

a. We need to recognise the differences between non-negotiables and negotiables, i.e. between the unchangeable (principles) and changeable (practices, methods, strategies).

b. We need to cultivate readiness for new light, borne of an enquiring spirit which is fed by the discipline of reading that takes us into fresh country. (Reading that stretches.)

c. Seek a sensitivity to the Holy Spirit who is always fresh and who can lead us into new things. We need to be saved from thinking that 'traditional' = 'spiritual'. (Exercise: list the number of new things the Holy Spirit did in the Book of Acts.)

d. Recognise that change is uncomfortable and goes against our predilection for security. Team members are going to need help in order to cope with change.

e. Change is going on around us all the time. We need insight to *recognise new factors* in our situation that must be reckoned

87

with and accommodated. This will then lead to *identifying new directions* for the team.

f. Recognise from the start the need for a way of coping with resistance. The number of people who resist change always outnumber those who see the need for it. Be ready for an uphill battle. Machiavelli wrote: *There is nothing more difficult to carry out nor more doubtful of success nor more dangerous to handle than to initiate a new order of things*.

g. Recognise the usefulness of *discontent*. There is an unspiritual discontent – murmuring. But there is a healthy discontent that is the seedbed of new and worthwhile ideas. Examples of justifiable discontent: a dissatisfaction with methods that are no longer productive; activities that are wasteful of time, human energy and money; availability of new technology that is not being used. Make discontent productive.

5. How to go about achieving change

a. Identify the factors that make change necessary and be able to explain them.

b. Extrapolate the situation five to ten years from now if you *don't* change. Evaluate the consequences.

c. Recognise that change is difficult. Have arguments strong enough to overcome resistance.

d. Give people time to consider change. Give plenty of notice about when a discussion on change will take place.

e. Keep your vision *big* and aim *low*. Do not go for sudden, sweeping change. Move slowly and work with those most likely to be affected.

f. Spot and enlist the help of those who can see that change is vital.

g. Take pains to clarify and communicate these factors:

- The *extent* of the change.
- The *rate* of change.
- *Who* will be involved.
- The *results* of the change.
- *Method* of implementing the change.
- *Timing* of the change.
- *Who* will be responsible.
- *How* a change will be monitored.

h. Begin the change at the place where the most control can be exercised.
i. Be on hand to monitor/adjust/substitute/remedy/cancel.
j. An idea for change may have to be 'rescued' from the person proposing it and given to an astute group who can reshape it in acceptable form.
k. Involve the maximum number of people in the decision-making process relevant to the change so that they are motivated to see it accomplished successfully.
l. Constantly seek to create a positive climate for the change you see is needed. Accentuate the positive.

6. Coping with resistance to change

a. Identify all obstacles to change (people, circumstances, costs, present practices).
b. Well ahead of change be prepared to spend time and energy giving detailed explanations to those who are most likely to oppose.
c. Learn how to 'unfreeze' people's attitude by having a warm, positive attitude yourself. Diagnose whether the opposition is to the idea or to you personally.

d. Have answers ready for the following standard objections:

- This may set a precedent.

- It will cost more.

- This isn't the time to try it.

- We've never done it this way before.

- It's just a fad; it'll pass.

- We've managed without it up till now.

- We don't have the money/expertise/personnel/ equipment/ facilities ... to do it.

e. Always try to discover, and meet, the true reasons why a proposed change is resisted. Some possibilities:

- A genuine assessment that the change won't produce any better results than at present.

- A real fear of the unknown.

- Mistrust of the motive behind introducing the change.

- Interpreting change as a judgement on the previous method, or on the persons who set it up.

- A person's assumption that he/she will not have the capacity to do things differently.

- A dislike, not so much of the change proposed, but of the ramifications of it, such as:

  - being shifted to work with less amenable co-workers.

  - having to change one's location.

  - being assigned to another sub-team.

  - personal factors having to be rearranged (family considerations, holidays, personal costs, etc.).

f. The leader should prepare a diagram that clearly identifies the weaknesses of the present situation, the new changes, the immediate advantages and how this will affect the goals.

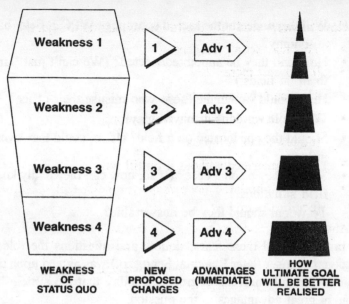

| WEAKNESS OF STATUS QUO | NEW PROPOSED CHANGES | ADVANTAGES (IMMEDIATE) | HOW ULTIMATE GOAL WILL BE BETTER REALISED |

Historical note

Perhaps a word of testimony (history!) may help at this point. At a gathering of WEC leaders the writer suggested that the main cause of the breakdown in health of two of our International Secretaries was the fact that WEC had no intermediate leadership problem-solving structure. We had the International Secretary and then we had field, base, and ministry leaders. We desperately needed another level – those who could be 'big brothers' to groups of fields.

Because of the obvious need for change there was very little serious opposition to the concept, but there were issues that had to be faced such as:

- Where were these 'super' leaders going to come from?
- If we took them from existing operations would we not defeat our field goals?
- How could their function be financed?
- We have managed up till now. Why change?
- What authority will they have?

91

- Will this undercut the sacred concept of WEC'S field/ base autonomy?
- How will they be appointed/elected? (We can't just 'land' them on fields.)
- How would we handle those who misuse their office?
- What role would their wives play?
- Should they be located on a field? (If so, could they overly influence it?)
- Should they be on a base? (If so, how can they really know field situations?)
- To whom should they be answerable?

In spite of all these fears, doubts and questions the role of Regional Adviser (later Regional Secretary) was agreed upon and there is virtually universal agreement today that the system has brought great advantages to the mission.

Questions for study and discussion

1. Study the reactions of the spies who reconnoitred the promised land, and the people's reactions to their report.
   Can you spot some of the items listed in the two columns in section I?
2. What should a leader do if he faces massive opposition to change, in the majority of his team?
3. Talented people are sometimes 'spiky' people. What does this call for in the leader? How far should he 'go along' with them?

Bibliography

P. Crosby, *The Art of Getting Your Own Sweet Way* (New York, USA: McGraw Hill, 1972)

E. Griffen, *The Mind Changers* (Wheaton, IL: Tyndale, 1976)

B. Powers, *Christian Leadership* (Nashville, TN: Broadview Press, 1979)

10

The Biggest Battle

Let's face it. Without a vital personal prayer life a leader's ministry is powerless. He may go through the motions of leading but his ministry as a leader will be ineffective. There have been many leaders in WEC who have had serious limitations – but they have been men of prayer and God has anointed and blessed their leadership.

Those of us who were present could never forget David Macmillan's message at Intercon 90 when he ministered to us on the 'needing friend', the 'pleading friend', and the 'feeding friend' in Luke 11:5-10. What struck us all was not merely the incisiveness of his analysis, the effectiveness of his application, but the fact that he was speaking out of his experience of prayer and intercession in the Thailand field.

1. The personal prayer life

The diagram below summarises the various kinds of praying found in the Bible. The outer rim indicates the objectives of our praying. The segments 1 to 7 represent the style of prayer required for these objectives. The hub recognises the supreme enabling role of the Holy Spirit.

All seven prayer styles can be exercised both on a private and corporate level, but 2 to 5 are mainly used in private and 1, 6 and 7 are generally used in group praying.

Worship and praise (segment 1 in diagram 1) is normally directed to the Lord. Thanksgiving (segment 2 in diagram 1) can also be in recognition of the Lord's goodness and grace, but it can be expressed for situations, events and people as well.

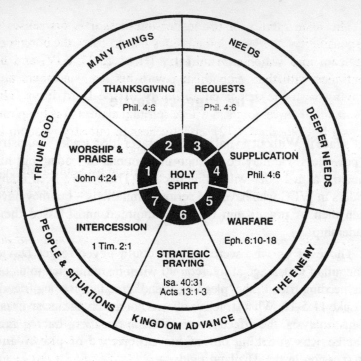

Diagram 1

Request (segment 3 in diagram 1) is a simple asking, but supplication is earnest entreaty and is more intense.

The greatest personal challenge to any leader is at the level of intercession (segment 7 in diagram 1). Study the lives of great leaders in the Bible and you will detect an inner ministry of travail in prayer on behalf of those for whom they are responsible:

- the Lord Jesus   John 17
- Moses   Exod. 14:15; 32:31-32; 33:9-14
- Daniel   Dan. 2:18-20; 6:10; 9:4-23; 10:7-14
- Samuel   1 Sam. 7:5,8-9; 8:6,21; 12:18, 19,23.

The main quality of the leader-intercessor is his sense of responsibility. The Lord commissions him to carry the burden of his team in a watch-care ministry (Heb. 13:17 KJV) and he continues with that, empathising with his team members and praying with the delegated authority of the Lord Jesus. His objectives in prayer for them will be spiritual maturity (as Epaphras prayed in Colossians 4:12), effectiveness in ministry, wisdom in relationships, and a sense of direction and strategy.

The following are extracts from an article by Samuel Mateer, a missionary in Ecuador on the subject 'Prayer as Part of Your Working Day':

My home church taught me to pray in daily devotions but not much else. Missionaries surveyed in Quito said they spent 20 minutes in prayer a day! Ministry prayer is something different. It is praying during the working day as part of your ministry. Prayer is not only for the work of the church, it is the work of the church. Ministry prayer is extended prayer. Jesus spent nights in prayer and prayed often during the day (Luke 5:16). We live in a frightful world where Satan could hold up Daniel's prayer for 21 days (Dan. 10:12). Ministry prayer keeps us on an even keel. Lack of ministry prayer contributes to missionary attrition.

Set goals – and pray for them. Prayer is action. Prayer is ministry: we must not feel guilty about taking work hours to pray. Part of our ministry is to encourage others to pray this way. We stretch them to goals beyond themselves. As they pray they find a ministry, and this puts new meaning into their lives.

Once when I focussed my prayers on an elder-elect and his negative spirit, he began to change. But he really changed when he caught the vision that he could pray for the church rather than criticise it. Fasting and prayer go together in Scripture. We have to deal not only with our attitude but also our priorities. All of us find time for what we consider important. Time can be found for prayer, days can be set aside for fasting. If we are really convinced that this is what God wants us to do, we will do it.

The married leader should develop a joint prayer ministry with his wife on behalf of the team, and if his deputy (and his wife) are available the four should develop a joint intercessory role as much as is practicable. Single leaders should develop a prayer ministry with their co-leader or deputy leader.

2. Strategic praying as a team exercise

The art of strategic praying (segment 6) needs to be re-emphasised in all our bases and fields. This is the exercise of waiting on God for the discernment of His purposes and then praying through to faith about what He has revealed. It is described in one of Norman Grubb's early books *Touching the Invisible*, pp. 9-11. The sequence of events can be summarised as follows:

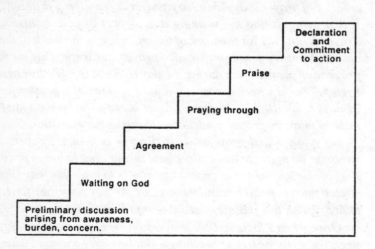

Diagram 2

a. Preliminary discussion

The group becomes aware of, or burdened for, a situation that causes concern. The matter will probably be raised by the leader. The group examines the problem from various angles, ensuring all necessary information is to hand that can shed light on it. (A scriptural principle? A mission manual? Mission guidelines?)

b. Waiting on God

In line with Isaiah 40:31 the group takes time to *wait* in God's presence (not asking for anything other than light and understanding) so that it can see the situation from the perspective of the throne. This is exercising our ministry as 'kingly priests' (1 Pet. 2:9).

c. Agreement

It is amazing how the teaching of Matthew 18:19 – on the necessity for reaching agreement – is ignored! We need time to discuss and to reach agreement about what the objective of our believing should be. ('Agree' = *sumphoneo* = sound together.)

d. Praying through

This is the mystery section! We know God does not have to be persuaded, yet there is this need for 'praying through' to a point of absolute faith. (Is its real purpose to deliver us from unbelief ?)

e. Praise

At some point the burden lifts. Prayer turns to praise and delight at the prospect of the fulfilment of God's revealed purpose.

f. Declaration and Commitment to Action

We finally 'go over the top' with 'public declaration' of what God is going to do. It puts us 'out on a limb' – but that is how we prove God.

And we commit ourselves to action in line with the declaration even though material guarantees are non-existent.

3. Spiritual Warfare (segment 5 in diagram 1)

It often happens that a leader under a huge workload feels it is legitimate to delegate leadership of the 'prayer times'. This writer suggests that it is in this very area that he should be maximising his leadership role. If the leader does not take the lead in spiritual warfare not a great deal will be achieved in the long term.

There appear to be three main lines in which the leader should have a dynamic contribution:

- *Recognising* and *revealing*. He has to be able to discern the enemy at work and to reveal this to the group.

- *Rallying* and *resisting*, by giving a call for unity in prayer and setting the tone by resisting and binding forces of evil.

- *Relying* on *resources*. He must exercise a ministry by teaching and by example as to how available resources are to be used.

Matthew 12:29 is a very revealing verse which clearly draws attention to *priorities* in spiritual warfare.

How can anyone enter a strong man's house and carry off his possessions unless he first ties up the strong man? Then he can rob his house.

It seems that in many situations well-intentioned workers have tried to rob Satan's house *without* carrying out the *initial* and necessary *binding* of the enemy.

Noel Gibson (formerly of Open Air Campaigners, now exercising an outstanding ministry in Australia) writes:

I was teaching discipleship in Korea. While praying for one of the female students, the Lord clearly said to me, 'Break cultural bondages.' Without understanding what this meant, but in simple obedience I used the authority of the name of Jesus and broke the young lady's cultural bondages. As soon as I had finished praying she jumped up and hugged me. This seemed to be out of character for anyone of her racial background, but each student

with whom I prayed showed the same reaction. ... The next coun-
try where I obeyed the Lord's same instruction was Japan. The
numbers were greater and the results even warmer. During this
time the Lord began to give understanding about the bondages
and dominations caused by Japanese culture, ancestor worship,
and religious spirits. From that time onwards I always prayed
for Japanese nationals to be released from these spirits before
commencing to lead them to Christ.

Are we formulating strategies that take into account the necessity for binding and breaking the grip of these Satanic forces
first?

Unfortunately, there is much praying *around* but little *pray-*
ing through. One cause of this is lack of dynamic leadership which
can hold the group to agreed goals; another is lack of knowledge
about our resources. What are these resources?

- Vocalised praise (2 Chron. 20:21-23, Acts 16:25-32).
- The power of the blood of Jesus (Rev. 12:11; 1 John 3:8).
  (The efficacy of the Death of Jesus.)
- The authority of the name of Jesus (Acts 3:6; 16:18).
- The full armour of God (Eph. 6:12-17).
- Overcoming faith (1 John 5:4; Rom. 8:37; 1 Pet. 5:9).
- The applied and relevant Word of the Lord (Acts 4:31; 2:42-47).
- All kinds of prayer (Eph. 6:18).

It is not enough to bring God our shopping list; we need to see
the dynamics of strategic faith and overcoming faith. It is
'according to our faith' not 'according to our asking' that things
will be done.

Much praying is carried out in small groups – and there is a
place for this – but it is in the well-led large group that direction
can be found, discipline (in maintaining an agreed line) exercised,
and declarations of faith reached. And the leader is the one to do it.

Questions for study and discussion

1. Evaluate your team's awareness and readiness for spiritual conflict. What needs to be done?
2. Could this subject be a matter for discussion at the annual conference or for a special seminar?
3. How do you go about reaching 'agreement' within your group, before praying?

Bibliography

D. Burnett, *Unearthly Powers* (Eastbourne UK: MARC Europe, 1988)

E. Crossman, *Mountain Rain* (Singapore: OMF, 1982)

J. Dawson, *Taking our Cities for God* (Waco, TX: Word, 1989)

R. Foster, *Prayer: Finding the Heart's True Home* (London, UK: Hodder and Stoughton, 1992)

N. Gibson, *Evicting Demonic Squatters & Breaking Bondages* (Drummoyne, NSW, Aust.: Freedom in Christ Ministries, 1987)

N. Grubb, *Rees Howells, Intercessor* (London, UK: Lutterworth (& Ft. Washington, USA: CLC) 1952)

N. Grubb, *Touching the Invisible* (London, UK: Lutterworth, 1940)

G. MacDonald, *Ordering Your Private World* (Crawborough, UK: Highland Books, 1985)

A. Matthews, *Born for Battle* (Singapore: OMF, 1978)

C.P. Wagner & E.D. Pennoyer, *Wrestling with Dark Angels* (Ventura CA: Regal, 1990)

P. Wagner, *Territorial Spirits* (Chichester, UK: Sovereign World, 1991)

P. Wagner, *Warfare Prayer* (Ventura, CA: Regal, 1992)

SECTION 4
PERSONAL ISSUES

11

Excellence

'Success hinges upon a passion for excellence' (J.F. Kennedy). What are marks of excellence in a leader? In a sense this whole book is an attempt to answer that question. However, a number of unique qualities come to mind that are worthy of emphasis or re-emphasis in this chapter.

1. Competence

The challenge of competence comes at two levels. Do you have a firm enough attitude regarding standards for yourself? And do you have the courage to seek high standards of competence in the members of your team?

What steps are you taking to improve your personal competence in some area within the sphere of your total responsibility? Here is a formula for self improvement:

a. 'I will reserve the following dates and times for a personal improvement programme.'

b. 'I will plan to attend a seminar on ... When? Where?'

c. 'I will start reading leadership literature ... What? When?'

d. 'I will analyse my own use of time. This is how I will do it ...'

e. 'The area which has the greatest possibility for improvement is ... I will start there. What? How? When?'

What can you do to improve the standards of your team's performance? Can a mission like WEC have *quality control*? Ted Engstrom says:

*Christian organisations ... attach some nebulous kind of spiritual
aura to performance and workmanship. Because they ... feel it is
a matter between the worker and the Lord they often fail to
demand excellence and to challenge (workers) to strive for it,
feeling that some work, or inferior work is better than none. So
most groups dare not have a high expectation level of
performance.*

Is this not a special danger where we are all unpaid volunteers
in the organisational sense? Are we thereby inhibited from
expecting and encouraging excellence?

Of course, handling such issues makes the maximum demand
on our own spiritual wisdom, tact and diplomacy. Often we have
to make the agonising choice between peace and containment on
the one hand and the good of the fellowship and the standard of
the work on the other. As leaders we can be downright cowards!
And when this happens, not only does the work suffer – individuals do not reach the zenith of their competence.

2. Creativity

The longer we continue to do a thing in a certain way, the less
likely we are to think of other (and better) ways of doing it. From
that angle, experience becomes a *curse* rather than a *blessing*.

Of course, one could argue that 'experience' implies that we
have tried other ways, and the way we are doing it now is the
best. This seems to place experience in a stronger position than
innocence, but then we have no guarantee that experience has
discovered *all* the ways of doing it. The eventuality of finding a
better way continues to exist. Some of the implications of all this
are interesting:

a. The longer one method is used, the more it becomes a structure
   of security for those using it. The known is always more
   comfortable than the unknown. Repetition is far easier than

103

change. It is far easier to defend the status quo than move in new ways.

b. A newcomer in our ranks might just be able to suggest a better way than what has been used hitherto.

c. The innocent newcomer is much more sensitive to ultimate objectives than the experienced. His head is still up, looking around, whereas the experienced person's head is down, getting on with it. The newcomer may also be benefitting from better training methods and later technologies than a more senior person.

All this is not to denigrate traditional methods or undermine the value of experienced workers. The purpose is simply to appeal to all for a greater openness and generosity of spirit to any creative thinkers whom God may direct into our ranks and to warn of the dangers of 'hardened arteries' (fixed concepts and procedures). Consider the following examples from recent WEC history:

- Capital city A in Africa field B was reckoned to be a place where open-air meetings (in a Muslim society) were a 'no-no'. But a new indigenous African mission came in and did it, reaping much fruit.

- Field C concentrated on medical work but had minimal fruit. New workers explored other ways of serving the people which were less demanding physically and gave more opportunity for communication. Result: much greater fruitfulness.

- Workers in a hard field E used standard techniques of evangelism for years with limited results. A new couple got the OK to rent a home near a university town and use it as a 'drop-in' hospitality centre for friendship evangelism. Result: greater fruitfulness through closer social contact.

3. Empathy

Empathy is defined in the dictionary as 'a mental entering into the feeling or spirit of a person', 'the power of entering into another's personality and imaginatively experiencing his experience'.

Here is a check-list of questions to face up to what are the practical realities of empathy:

a. Does my relationship extend further than that required by my official position?

b. Do I really know the quality of my team members' relationship with the Lord, their spouse, their children?

c. Can I detect the signs of hurt, frustration, discouragement?

d. Do I know the hopes and aspirations held for their ministry?

e. Am I up to date in my assessment of their progress in their ministry?

f. Am I spending sufficient time with them so as to be able to answer these questions?

g. Have I a sufficiently accurate evaluation of their gifts and skills so that I can match these with the tasks to be done?

h. Have I a satisfactory grasp of their *capacity* so that they are carrying a workload suitable to that capacity?

i. Have I ensured that personalities in the sub-team to which they are allotted are compatible?

j. Are the overall objectives of the team resting easily with each member of it?

A.W.Tozer, in describing Robert Jaffray who pioneered the gospel in Viet Nam, writes:

Nothing can take the place of affection. Those who have it in generous measure have a magic power over men. Intellect will not do. Bible knowledge is not enough. Jaffray loved people for their own sakes. Are we developing our capacity for friendship? Should a good leader not also be a good friend?

4. Magnanimity (in this context, readiness to accept criticism)

'Yes-men are your enemies' (Solzhenitsyn).

Criticism is *healthy*. It is a safety valve for the fellowship (so don't close the valve!) and helps keep the lines clear between us.

Criticism is *necessary*. We need it. Iron sharpens iron; we should all be catalysts for each other's personal development, and this increases our effectiveness.

Rightly handled, criticism has a positive effect! It results in the removal of hindrances and weaknesses and enables us to function more in line with our goals. (The first draft of this book was circulated to thirty WEC leaders, asking for comments. Result: Thirty A4 sheets of suggestions, most of which have been incorporated.)

The word 'criticism' comes from *krino*, meaning to judge. It is obvious that the essential ingredient is evaluation or appraisal; it is non-moral. We all have to evaluate to stay alive. (Can I overtake before that bus comes through?) Discernment can turn into a critical attitude, which is negative and destructive. ('A, you really blew it in your handling of B ...') But this needn't be so. Discernment – even when its valuations are negative – *need not* be *destructively* critical; you can be *constructively* critical. ('Look, A, I feel you could have handled B a better way ...')

If someone comes to you (as leader) with a criticism, you can bet your bottom dollar that it is done only after a good bit of thought. No one wants to be in the leader's bad books. So:

a. Be prepared to think through the issue from the criticiser's angle. There must be some reason for his coming. Find it and don't be touchy.
b. Analyse the *reason* for the criticism. Is it *valid*, even though you don't immediately have an answer to the criticism?

c. Explain your *decisions* but don't defend *yourself*. A reasonable person accepts reasons. A dogmatic one-eyed person relishes a fight, and that's what you'll have on your hands if you defend yourself.

d. If necessary, *ask for time* to think through the issue presented if no satisfactory explanation can be given on the spot. Asking for time is also a good cooling-off device.

e. Ensure your reaction is not *person*-oriented but *truth*-oriented.

f. Most probably the criticiser doesn't want to hurt you so don't look on criticism as an insult.

g. Don't interpret any desire for change from the status quo as back-handed criticism.

h. Do recognise that younger workers have different value systems, lifestyles, and social mores (even those from your own homeland).

i. Do recognise that freedom to express criticism is *cultivated* in the educational systems of many countries. Questioning is not rebellion – it is today's way of thinking a thing through.

j. Develop a 'safety-valve' mechanism which makes it easy for someone who has a genuine 'gripe' to contact you personally.

5. Productivity

Our biggest danger is being concerned about *maintaining* rather than *achieving*; about doing things right, rather than doing the right thing; about tinkering with the machinery rather than turning out the product. Most of our time in staff conferences is taken up with machinery matters (personnel and work problems, procedures, administration, elections, committees, reports, etc.) rather than *evaluating* our effectiveness and evolving better methods. We gravitate to dealing with the 'urgent' rather than the strategic. ... So how can we change the emphasis? Here are some suggestions:

a. Accurately match gifting to task

Leaders must accept the absolute need for knowing every worker's gift/s and for liberating them to achieve that for which they are gifted. (For 'gifted' read 'divinely designed'.)

Perhaps a little WEC history will help. Norman Grubb was a master at spotting giftedness and putting it to work. Take his secretary – Fred Anthony. He could keep his mouth shut and turn out a perfect letter. Fred was not a fellowship man or a spiritual giant, but he was worth his weight in gold. Pat Symes was a colossus of faith, sacrifice and tenacity and was the true founder of our Colombian work. But he had constant fellowship problems; Grubb had to pay several visits to sort things out. But he backed Pat to the hilt because of his productiveness. Leslie Brierley became WEC's first Research Secretary because his findings and proposals were absolutely strategic in Grubb's eyes. He saw that adequate research was the key to the future. Leslie could have done other jobs in WEC – he was Field Leader of Guinea-Bissau for a time – but Grubb cashed in on his outstanding gift. In the Rowbothams Grubb saw a couple of homemakers with a gift of faith. They were not intellectuals, or preachers, or super-counsellors, yet they were let loose to develop a Scottish HQ which eventually became the first WEC Missionary Training College. Heini Germann-Edey was an initiator. He was not an administrator, but he could get things started. There would have been no Kalbar field, no Indonesian Missionary Fellowship (IMF), no Batu Bible School but for him. Grubb backed him, but WEC could not cope with his individualism and asked him to resign!

b. Make strength productive

Peter Drucker in *The Effective Executive* (Pan Books, London, 1966) writes:

> *The effective executive makes strength productive. He knows that one cannot build on weaknesses. To achieve results, one has to*

use all available strengths. These strengths are the true opportunities. Strong people always have strong weaknesses too. Where there are peaks there are valleys. There is no better prescription for executive effectiveness than the words Andrew Carnegie chose for his own tombstone: 'Here lies a man who knew how to bring into his service men better than himself.'

c. Productivity is largely dependent on personality

Productivity depends as much on the leader's charisma as upon his commitment, upon his personality as upon his person, upon his giftedness as upon his goal concentration.

We can become almost clinical and computerlike in pursuing goals yet the ship can lose momentum simply because the leader's personality does not evoke loyalty, enthusiasm and commitment; position and persuasiveness are out of balance. We need stature in the eyes of others as well as status. What can be done in this area?

Listen to what the people tell you about yourself, and make it easy for them to do so. Be vulnerable.

Have on your committee those who are willing to be absolutely open with you.

Don't build a defensive posture by being a 'desk man' exclusively. Cultivate interaction and a consultative style.

Pray with at least one other person about your limitations.

Have a known mechanism whereby comments, complaints, and criticisms can be heard and handled expeditiously.

Be as rigid as you like on *principles* but flexible on *methods* – and know the difference.

d. Prayer – the powerhouse behind productivity

When will we start to take seriously the Lord's requirement in Matthew 18:19-20, that we *agree* before praying, as a group? The usual procedure is simply to announce the matters for prayer and then proceed to pray. Jesus says we must take time to *reach a consensus*. Consensus is the key and discussion must precede it so that all can come to oneness of mind regarding the Lord's will in a situation. Please re-read *Touching the Invisible* by Norman Grubb. It is foundational stuff.

Another aspect of united prayer is simply that the greater the number of people praying together the more effective that prayer is. Do our field and sending base arrangements take into account that the spiritual conflict is far better handled in sizeable groups than in isolated ones, twos, or threes? Unbelief thrives in isolation. Here is a quotation from the page of a book that someone sent me recently in the mail. Unfortunately the name of the book or author was not included:

> *Both Scripture and contemporary experience indicate that there is a cumulative power in united praying. It was at a united prayer meeting that the mighty power of Pentecost was unleashed (Acts 2:1,2). It was when the believers 'lifted up their voices to God' that the place was shaken (Acts 4:24,31). It was the prayer of the whole church that secured Peter's release (Acts 12:5). The missionary church had its birth in a united prayer meeting (Acts 13:1-4).*

See Chapter 10 on Strategic Prayer.

6. Tenacity (having and maintaining a sense of direction)

The word 'administration' (NIV) is from *kubernesis*, from *kubernao* to guide, steer. *Kubernetes* is the pilot of a ship (Acts 27:11). The good leader (administrator) will have a *strong sense of direction* as far as his team's ministries are concerned. See Chapter 8 on Vision, Goals and Strategy for further details on this.

Here are a few questions about this area to which the leader should be able to give clear answers:

a. Where are we?

At what stage are we in our progress to agreed objectives? Are we where we *ought* to be?

b. Where will we get to, if we go on as we are?

This question highlights the ultimate effectiveness or otherwise of current activities.

c. Where should we be going?

This faces us with our overall sense of purpose. Do we have agreed, measurable sub-goals leading to the main objective?

d. Why should we be going there?

This makes us face up to our basic philosophy of mission – the very reason for our existence as an operational unit.

e. What do we need in order to go there?

This will help us to sharpen our evaluation of our resources and what more is needed by way of manpower, finances, property, transport, etc.

f. What is excess baggage?

What is being done that is tangential – not contributing to the agreed objectives?

g. What needs to change?

The answer to this can be in terms of of adjusted vision, attitudes, expectancy, spiritual warfare, levels of co-operation with other groups/national church, ministries or ministry methods.

h. When do we reckon to achieve our objectives?

This helps us to sharpen up our faith focus for eventual accomplishment of our task. This is crucial in the area of transfer of responsibility to nationals.

Two of the leader's dangers are *loss of momentum* and *deflection*.

Contributing factors are:

- Unwillingness to delegate. You are coach of a team, not driver of a busload of passengers. (See Chapter 6.)
- Unwillingness for the insecurity of change. (See Chapter 9 on Change.)
- Too much time taken problem solving. (Problem solving is good but it does not advance the work – it only clears away clutter.)
- Being too available. Availability is good – but not *constant* availability. Time must be given to *productive* activity.

7. A positive attitude

Here are some DO's and DONT'S that will help cultivate a right attitude in the leader. They are largely influenced by Robert Schuller's book *You Can Be the Person You Want To Be*.

a. Your consistent attitude will fundamentally affect the outcome of every team task.
b. Your positive attitude will have the effect of helping other team members be positive.
c. Approach every person with a positive appraisal and appreciation of his strengths. Make strength productive.
d. Let your attitude show that the person you are dealing with is needed, appreciated, and important for the success of the whole work.
e. When ideas and suggestions are offered, dismiss from your mind the negative response and try to see the positive value of it.

Now for the warnings:

a. Never block a helpful suggestion because it entails difficulties.
b. Never oppose something because it has never been done before and you can't imagine how it can be done.
c. Never oppose a potentially good suggestion just because some part of it is not right.
d. Never let lack of time, money, brains, energy, talent or skills be the ultimate reason for turning down a proposition.
e. Never broadcast negative comments about others.

Take a good hard look at your current mental outlook. Honestly now, are you *problem*-oriented, or *possibility*-oriented? Of course leadership must be involved in problem solving, but if you do not lead the field in *possibility* thinking you will never motivate your team to maximum productiveness. Schuller describes how his whole lifestyle changed when he took this verse to heart: 'Be confident in this one thing that God who has begun a good work in you will complete it [He will give you strength and skill to succeed]'. To this we might add Philippians 2:13: 'For it is God who works in you to will and to act according to his good purpose.' Paul writes to Timothy: 'God has not given you the spirit of fear but of power [ability to achieve – *dunamis*], love and a renewed mind' (2 Tim.1:7). And the writer to the Hebrews says: 'May the God of peace ... equip you with everything good for doing his will that he may work in us what is pleasing to him' (Heb. 13:20-21).

The life story of John Hyde of India (*Praying Hyde*) has an incident with a valuable lesson.

There was another missionary on the field who was difficult to work with. One day Hyde was praying for him and telling God all about this man's faults. Then he sensed the Lord was closing his lips and was saying, 'Praise Me for the evidences of grace in his life.' So Hyde started to praise God for that person – his willingness to come to India, his tenacity in spite of satanic opposition, his love for the people, etc.

When Hyde met up with him a month later he was a changed person. 'You're different,' said Hyde. 'Yes,' the other man said. 'One day, a month ago, the Lord dealt with me in a remarkable way and I've been different ever since.'

Questions for study and discussion

1. Is your field/SB strategy being frequently updated? Describe some changes made in the last three years.
2. Do you see any dangers in the 'make-strength-productive' theory of Peter Drucker?
3. How can you be positive about negative people?

Bibliography

T. Peters and R. Waterman, *In Search of Excellence* (New York, USA: Warne, 1982)

R. Schuller, *The Peak to Peek Principle* (New York, USA: Doubleday/Bantam, 1980)

J. White, *Excellence in Leadership* (Leicester, UK: IVP, 1986)

12

Pitfalls Are Plentiful

1. Discouragement

'I am the subject of depressions of spirit so fearful that I hope none of you ever get to such extremes as I get to.' Is this some defeated worker speaking? No! It is none other than the prince of preachers, C.H. Spurgeon! So if you are a victim of depression or discouragement you are in good company – Abraham, Moses, Jonah, Peter, Luther, Calvin, Campbell Morgan and Andrew Bonar.

a. Causes could be physical/mental as well as spiritual. If you are emotionally, spiritually or physically drained – especially after a period of intense activity/ministry/counselling/travel – you are very susceptible. Such draining can only be rectified by rest and renewal. Use a circuit breaker such as a day off, physical exercise, listening to music, a game with the kids.

b. If discouragement comes from failure or ineffectiveness, seek to learn something positive out of it. Failure need never be final.

c. If you are at wit's end corner, just cry to the Lord. Literally cry. Tears may not change the circumstances, but they can change you. The Psalms can help (42, 51).

d. If discouragement has come through negative thinking (like self-pity) or critical thinking ('other people are so awful') recognise such indulgence as sin and take release through Calvary.

e. If there is someone you can talk to, and trust, meet with that person.

f. Recognise discouragement as a major activity of Satan.

Discouragement only comes from the devil. He distracts our attention from the resistless Name of Jesus to our own unworthiness. He is the master of the telephone, a baby pincher, a dog provoker, a bringer of useless visitors, a wife irritator. He can pour a smokescreen of evil and foul thoughts into the midst of a beautiful supplication. He directs our closest attention from the majesty of God to the aches and woes of our bodies. He can explain away all answers to prayer if given a chance and slanders both God and the brethren. His greatest trick is to get us into a direct fight with himself, thus bypassing Christ. He is the author of books which unintentionally magnify his power and forget his defeat, though they are supposedly designed to instruct us on how to resist him. He causes the church to call committee meetings each night and cracks the whip behind the frenzied religious activity of the day – smiling all the while at the empty prayer meetings. He is the greatest of all sidetrackers and time consumers. (Source unknown.)

2. Failure to confer or confront

Missionary A goes on furlough. After a few months he hears from the field leader that, owing to new conditions on the field, his ministry for the next term will be changed. He has not been consulted or given a chance to make any input into the changing situation. Is it any surprise that he battles over whether to return?

Senior missionary B has consistently upset new workers who have been placed with him, because of his dogmatism and inflexibility over methods. Yet the field leader has never sat down and squarely faced him up with this consistent pattern.

Motto 1: Never finalise a discussion without ensuring that all who are going to be affected by it are given an opportunity to express themselves.

116

Motto 2: Confrontation is known to cause more stress in Christian work than any other factor. Yet failure to confront causes untold suffering for those who feel the effect of the unchallenged brother's attitudes and actions. And the leader loses his standing through apparent weakness.

3. The temptation to be operative instead of executive

Operators *do* things. Executives concentrate on helping operators to do things but are wasted if they 'do' themselves. The primary task of the leader is to facilitate the work of others. No one else in the team can do that, and if it is not done the field/base is deprived of true leadership. The operator *adds*; the executive *multiplies*. The operator *achieves*; the executive *ensures* that others *achieve*.

The operator's satisfaction is a job well done; the executive's satisfaction is in knowing that many people are doing their jobs well.

The larger the team is, the more imperative it is for the leader to desist doing jobs that others should do.

There can be a bit of leeway when a team is small (6-10 or so) but as numbers grow his responsibility as a facilitator, pastor or organiser increases to the point where little else can be undertaken.

Don't dismiss the term 'executive' as irrelevant. It is simply the right term for the man or woman who services the team by ensuring that everything needed for members to accomplish the given task is in position. A multitude of factors determine this: location, accommodation, transport, money, relationships, skills, prayer, training, family needs, cultural adjustments, integration with nationals, ministry suitability, et cetera, et cetera. The leader is the service agent for others' effectiveness.

4. Burnout

There are a number of factors that bring a leader to this condition; here are some:

a. Using human resources instead of God's

If the calling of God is upon you for leadership then, biblically, it is right to expect the gifts that accompany the responsibility. The NIV version of Hebrews 13:20-21 is excellent, 'May the God of peace ... *equip you with everything good* for doing his will, and may *he work in us* what is pleasing to him, through Jesus Christ.'

As far as leadership in WEC is concerned, God has given new gifts to leaders for tasks in which hitherto they have had no experience or expertise. Others have failed because they did not trust God for the gifts needed, but tackled the job with human energy.

b. Carrying burdens only God can cope with

A worker has to be sent home. Another missionary couple are having marital problems. A national has been killed in a road accident. Mistrust has crept into church-mission relations ... Leaders who hold on to everything will soon find their knees buckling. They will eventually be crushed by the load. The more leaders care, the more they open themselves to others; the more effective they are, the more they are weighted down.

We are not constructed to carry all these burdens ourselves. We are meant to move them into the storehouse – the Lord. Don't reverse your function. You are not the storehouse! You are the storeman! Jesus says, 'Come to me all you who are weary and burdened and I will give you *rest.*' Carry the burden only long enough to give it to God.

c. Misplaced priorities

A pastor once wrote: 'To survive amid this reality (of having more to do than there is time for) I have cultivated the fine skill of

118

consecrated negligence. Perhaps this is my finest survival technique. Those who fail to learn it squirm in continual guilt or languish in chronic exhaustion.' The personal toll of being an 'ideal' leader is unbearable. The way to avoid this:

- Keep your objectives in sight.

- Have a recognised structure of priorities in the light of these and *stick to them*.

- Scrap the goal of perfection in every task. If you can get 90 per cent of the way in half the time, the remaining 10 per cent isn't worth 50 per cent of your time.

- Recognise your limitations (physical, mental, emotional) and live within them.

- Learn to say 'no', for the right reason.

- Avoid negative people and people who constantly drain you.

- Have a technique for recharging your physical batteries – a day/half day away from everything, a stimulating book, a visit with 'safe' friends, a mountain climb, a couple of hours with some music cassettes.

- Above all do what you have to do to maintain real sensitivity to the Lord.

5. Finally: how not to lose one's cutting edge

a. Here is a quotation from John Silk, International Secretary of our sister mission, Christian Literature Crusade. He wrote the following in 1986 (and was still steaming on as *is* when this was written in 1993).

I find it essential to develop an 'aloneness' with God. Times when I break into the normal schedule and soak myself in reading, tapes or walking/talking with the Lord. Work pressure convinces us that it is suicidal to take 'time off', yet the very opposite is true. It is suicide not to take 'time off'. Suicide not just for the leader, but for the led. We owe it to God and our teams to ensure that we are recharging the batteries. It may mean signing up for that retreat, buying a book, listening to tapes. Satan convinces us that this is a luxury, because he knows it is our very lifeline. Leadership is lonely, strenuous, exacting. It is all too easy to lose the cutting edge, to run out of steam.

b. The following points on *how to avoid burnout* appeared in *Life Ministries* magazine, (PO Box 200, San Dimas, CA 91773).

- Self-awareness.

- Learn to rest and relax regularly.

- Develop a support group – people you can pray with and confide in.

- Admit and recognise your weaknesses and learn how to deal with them.

- Set aside time for worship and refreshment.

- Learn to say 'no'. Don't overload your programme.

- Diminish the intensity of your lifestyle. Change what can be changed.

- If you think you're heading for burnout, get help.

- Take care of your body. Get regular exercise.

- Keep your sense of humour.

Questions for study and discussion

1. Can you identify with any of the pitfalls listed? Work out a course of action that will enable you to avoid them.

2. Work back from the premise 'God won't give you more to do than you have time for' and decide what, in your life, is not God-given.

3. How can one avoid the mistake of making the things we like to do our first priority?

4. 'Graveyards are full of people who were once indispensable.' What does this say to you?

5. Perfectionism – a curse or a blessing?

Bibliography

L. Ahlem, *Living with Stress* (Ventura, CA: Regal, 1978)

G. MacDonald, *Restoring Your Spiritual Passion* (Crowborough, UK: Highland Books (British Ed), 1986)

J. White, *Excellence in Leadership* (Leicester, UK: IVP (British Ed), 1986)

13

Stress

Stress is what the personality experiences when having to face and cope with a situation of demand, pressure, challenge or threat. Note the sequence in Romans 5:3-5: 'Suffering produces perseverance; perseverance, character; and character, hope.' The word 'suffering' is *thlipsis* – which has the basic idea of pressure from outside. We can see that pressure, in this passage, has beneficial effects, so we must not say that all pressure is bad. Marjory Foyle in her book *Honourably Wounded* notes that Paul's experience of pressure in 2 Corinthians 4: 8-9 (being 'hard pressed, perplexed, persecuted') results in 'Christ's life being revealed in his body'.

1. Not all stress is bad

We need stress because it results in us summoning our resources to meet the challenge. Too little stress leaves us languid; too much stress, over too long a period, leads to burnout – the 'in' term for exhaustion.

The good and bad effects of stress on performance were first noted by two men, R.M. Yerkes and J.D. Dodson of the Harvard Physiological Laboratory, who noticed that as stress increases so do efficiency and performance. However, there is a point where, if the stress continues and increases, performance starts to decrease. This will vary from individual to individual.

A senior worker, now retired, came up to the writer one day with the following diagram (or a similar version of it) in his hands. 'Stewart,' he said, 'if I had had this three years ago I wouldn't be in the state I am in today.'

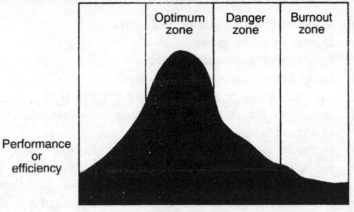

K. Sehnert in his book *Stress/Unstress* gives the following tabulation:

Not enough stress (underload)	Just the right amount	Too much stress (overload)
	RESULTS IN	
Boredom	Exhilaration	Insomnia
Apathy	High motivation	Irritability
Erratic sleep pattern	Mental alertness	Accidents
Decrease in motivation	High energy	Change in appetite
Lethargy	Realistic analysis of problems	Strained relationships
Negativity	Sharp perception	Increased amount of errors
Dullness	Calmness under pressure	Loss of perception Indecisiveness

Symptoms of over-stress are listed by Cecily Booth as follows:

a. More tired than normal or unable to sleep.
b. Overeat or lose appetite.
c. Lose temper more quickly.
d. Laugh less or much more than usual.
e. Cry more easily or never show any emotion at all.
f. Experience fear or anxiety more frequently than usual and as a result dream more.
g. Become more talkative and ramble on, or feel one's thoughts are being interrupted (can't think), speak hesitatingly, inappropriately, or stutter. Feel one is saying the wrong thing.
h. Become untidy, depressed, constantly discouraged and lose drive for work, or work constantly, never taking adequate time to stop, rest, think.
i. Desire to be with people all the time or develop a fear of being with people.
j. Complain more about the actions of others, feel rejected by them and even become preoccupied with imagining that the actions of certain people are against one.
k. Frequent headaches, back or stomach aches or pain, skin rashes and other functional disorders.
l. May suffer prolonged complications and infections after minor colds or lose resistance to infection and have one infection after another.

Note: We *all* experience *some* of these symptoms *sometimes* (in short bursts). It is the unusual over a *protracted period* which must be taken note of.

2. Sources of missionary stress

An article by Kelly and Michelle O'Donnell in *Evangelical Missions Quarterly*, Jan 1991 (one in a series of three), reports on three researches conducted on this subject.

a. In 1981 Cedric Johnson and David Penner surveyed fifty-five North American Protestant missions with over 100 staff overseas and found that the major problem areas were:

- relationships with other missionaries.

- cultural adjustment.

- managing stress.

- raising children.

- marital difficulties.

- financial pressures.

- loneliness.

b. Another study by Dorothy Gish in 1983 covering 549 missionaries from USA, Canada, UK, Australia resulted in the following tabulation of factors in descending order:

- Confronting others when necessary.

- Communicating across language/cultural barriers.

- Time and effort maintaining donor relationships.

- Amount of work.

- Work priorities.

- Time for personal study of the Word and prayer.

- Progress in my work.

- Need for pastoral care.

- Making decisions affecting others' lives.

- Need for confidant.

- Self-acceptance.

- Conflicts between my values and those of host culture.

- 'Gold-fish bowl' existence.

- Uncertainty about my future.

125

- Freedom to take time for myself.
- Extended family concerns.
- Frequent moving.

c. In 1987 Phil Parshall surveyed 390 missionaries on the subject of adjustment and spirituality, and found that the problem areas were:

- discouragement.
- frustration.
- maintaining an effective devotional life.
- the battle for spiritual victory.
- managing feelings of sexual lust.

Analysing the findings of the three researches, the O'Donnells have come up with a summary of seven main areas where vigilance is crucial. They call it the CHOPPSS model:

C	Cultural stress:	language learning, adjusting to target culture, having different ways of meeting basic needs, re-entry to our culture.
H	Human stress:	conflict with others, opposition within host culture, family responsibilities and pressures.
O	Organisational stress:	job satisfaction, red tape, mission policy, leadership styles, work pressures.
P	Physical stress:	illness, ageing, adjustments to climate and environment.
P	Psychological stress:	unresolved past tensions, inner conflicts, depression, boredom, mid-life crisis.
S	Support stress:	money, housing, retirement, limited secretarial help.
S	Spiritual stress:	maintaining adequate devotional life, spiritual warfare, subtle temptations.

3. Internal & external stress

Stress can also be classified as internal and external.

a. Internal

This is when the factors producing the stress stem from the victim's own character, conscience, or failures such as disobedience to the revealed will of God (Jonah), downright sinfulness (Judas), lust and a wrongful liaison (David).

b. External

The most common factors have already been listed but a couple of examples may clarify issues.

A new missionary couple were advised to 'live near to the people'. The acting field leader procured accommodation in the heart of a bazaar area. The noise was deafening. They did move away eventually, but they were so stressed out that they left the field.

Lack of team concern and support produces stress. A certain station in a West African field is distant from the other centres. Most couples allocated to that area have had ill-health or discouragement leading to resignation.

4. Fright, fight and flight

a. Fright

This is the immediate response to a demanding situation – running for the footpath when a fast moving vehicle suddenly appears, grabbing a toddler before he falls down a slope, etc.

All kinds of things happen in the physical realm – faster heartbeat, adrenalin pumping, sweating, faster breathing, etc.

b. Fight

The personality can learn to cope with increased demand or challenge. Before exams, students have an increased heart rate and blood pressure. Before a race, runners show signs of tension.

Continued stress in a leader – often caused by having to handle personnel problems – has to be 'fought' by taking some form of remedial action. This can take the form of a strenuous physical work-out – fast walking, running, swimming or a team game – or by a deliberate relaxation response involving physical rest in a comfortable position in a quiet environment, with deep breathing and an attitude of meditation or prayer.

Having a hobby that provides a total change of activity and of mental process is invaluable.

c. Flight

If stress increases and continues beyond the individual's capacity to cope there is only one answer – total removal from the situation until one recovers.

It is a sad fact that 'holding on' once a person has reached the far side of the curve opens the way to impaired judgement, poor decision making, physical exhaustion and sexual impropriety.

James P. Satterthwaite, MD, a medical missionary in Japan, wrote the following:

A professional person who gets too fatigued will either become immoral or depressed. We missionaries are not immune. Immorality can come in many different ways and one way it hits missionaries is in sex. Another more common way is a persecution complex, actual paranoia: feeling that you are being persecuted, that somebody is out to get you.

It behoves leaders – for the sake of their team, and for the sake of maximum effectiveness in their leadership role – to take adequate time for regular relaxation, rest, recreation and holiday.

The leader who constantly defies God's order of one day of rest in seven is courting disaster

5. How to deal with stress (points are not necessarily chronological)

a. Recognise the symptoms for what they are – warning flags indicating some change is *essential*.
b. Seek to identify the source or reasons for the stress.
c. Recognise that serious readjustment to your programme will have to be worked out.
d. Don't treat yourself as a guilty person. Everyone has a tolerance limit, and leaders face stresses that non-leaders don't.
e. Seek help from your spouse, another trusted confidant, your deputy leader, your committee, regional secretary, or professionally qualified person.
f. Review your load. If not withdrawing, what can, what can't be delegated? Is your deputy under-used?
g. Don't try to cope by working in sleep time. Things will get worse.
h. Do whatever you can to improve your physical wellbeing – diet, vitamins, exercise, rest.
i. If physically laid low avoid the temptation to get back into things too soon.
j. Review and re-adjust any imbalance in your lifestyle relative to work/family/devotional life/rest and recreation.
k. Review your wife's situation. Is she getting a fair deal? Is she suffering unnecessary tension?
l. Introduce a regular mentally unwinding activity – reading, Scrabble, artwork, garden, music, etc.
m. Deal with any of your own longstanding relationship problems – unforgiveness, resentment, jealousy. Walk in the light.

6. Handling stress in others

The points given under 4. can easily be adapted for application to others. It is important to save them from the 'guilt' of realising they are getting special attention. The major factor is to make them realise that all individuals have their own level of stress tolerance.

It is also obviously crucial for leaders to retain as close a link as circumstances will allow with team members so that they are able to detect signs of stress before the breaking point is reached. Adequate visitation (though expensive in terms of time, travel and money) is absolutely necessary – and this means more than rushed visits.

7. How vulnerable are you to stress?

The following test, based on purely secular factors, was developed by psychologists Lyle H. Miller and Alma Dell Smith of Boston University Medical Centre.

Score each time from 1 (almost always) to 5 (never), according to how much of the time each statement applies to you.

a.   I eat at least one hot, balanced meal a day.

b.   I get seven to eight hours sleep at least four nights a week.

c.   I give and receive affection regularly.

d.   I have at least one relative within 50 miles on whom I can rely.

e.   I exercise to the point of perspiration at least twice a week.

f.   I smoke less than half a pack of cigarettes a day.

g.   I take fewer than five alcoholic drinks a week.

h.   I am the appropriate weight for my height.

i.   I have an income adequate to meet basic expenses.

j.   I get strength from my religious beliefs.

k.   I regularly attend club or social activities.

l.   I have a network of friends and acquaintances.

m.   I have one or more friends to confide in about personal matters.

n.   I am in good health (including eyesight, hearing, teeth).

o.   I am able to speak openly about my feelings when angry or worried.

p.   I have regular conversations with the people I live with about domestic problems, e.g. chores, money and daily living issues.

q.   I do something for fun at least once a week.

r.   I am able to organise my time effectively.

s.   I drink fewer than three cups of coffee (or tea or cola) a day.

t.   I take quiet time for myself during the day.

                                          TOTAL

To get your score, add up the figures and subtract 20. Any number over 30 indicates a vulnerability to stress. You are seriously vulnerable if your score is between 50 and 75, and extremely vulnerable if it is over 75.

Questions for study and discussion

1. How did Jesus handle stress?
2. Identify any potential stress-producing factors in your situation, and prescribe a means of dealing with them.
3. How should the fact that all the members of your team have different stress-tolerances affect your treatment of them?
4. In the light of this chapter how do you interpret Paul's words, 'I can do everything through him who gives me strength.'

Bibliography

L. Ahlem, *Living with Stress* (Ventura, CA: Regal Books, 1978)

M. Foyle, *Honourably Wounded* (London, UK: MARC Europe, 1987)

D. Gish, *Sources of Missionary Stress* (Grantham, PA: Messiah College, 1983)

M. Lawson, *Facing Anxiety & Stress* (London, UK: Hodder & Stoughton, 1986)

K. & M. O'Donnell, *Stress can be Managed* (Wheaton, IL: EMQ article, Jan 91)

M. Rush, *Burn-out* (London, UK: Hodder & Stoughton, 1986)

K. Sehnert, *Stress/Unstress* (Minneapolis, USA: Augsberg, 1981)

14

The Wisdom of Leonard Moules

In 1974 the then International Secretary of WEC wrote a Leadership Manual. As there are probably very few copies still in existence, the following pages are included; they consist of extracts from Len's writings. They are penetrating, practical and precise. Although mission situations have changed enormously and some of Len's lessons are outdated, the principles certainly still apply.

Len always assumed that every leader was married! So there are places where the single leader needs to substitute for 'wife', 'co-leader' or 'assistant leader'.

1. On appointment to leadership

It has often been said that leaders are born, not made. But it is my belief that leaders are made more than they were ever born. Alan Norrish in *Christian Leadership* writes: 'Most of us were born little tyrants, and if we had been allowed our way, would have become big ones!' Leadership is largely a matter of training. A capacity grows with experience, and experience develops maturity and balance. This all from the human side, and is nothing unless completely taken in hand by the Holy Spirit. Leadership is a spiritual gift. (See 1 Cor. 12:28, 20th Century New Testament) – 'Capacity to Govern'. So seek the Lord for this anointing.

a. Do not get involved in a specialist project (radio, printing, et cetera) to the detriment of time for the leadership responsibilities.

b. Never write or communicate when emotionally tense.

c. First reactions are usually of the flesh! Second thoughts and feelings tend to be more spiritual!

d. Ask God for *vision*. You should see at least three years or more 'down the road'. Your field workers may only see a year or more ahead. Drip-feed your vision to them at suitable times. It is not always wise to disclose all you have had revealed to you – it may be misunderstood.

e. Remember – weep with those who weep. Rejoice with those who rejoice. Be in the forefront of the Spirit's dealings in brokenness and confession. Don't be known as one who never admits he is wrong or has never been heard to say, 'I'm sorry.'

f. Always recognise your wife as a co-worker in this responsibility
  - Never overlook and ignore a woman's intuition about people and problems!
  - Pray together for the team.
  - Women's counselling is best left to her at the outset; you may join later in the consultations.
  - Let your wife check some letters before sending, especially if you have tended to be 'hot under the collar' over the reason for writing.

g. Give time to think through the strategy and tactics of the work.
  - What are our field objectives?
  - How far are we along the road?
  - What are the hindrances?
  - How can we resolve them?
  - Are we trusting responsibility to nationals?
  - What and when should the next responsibility be transferred?

h. Prayerfully evaluate your workers:
  - Those needing constant encouragement.
  - Those solidly loyal and dependable.

- Those so often sickly. Why? Is it pathological, psychological or spiritual? What can we do to minister to them?
- Those who tend to be critical. Would a visit from time to time for open, frank chats help?
- Those having financial difficulties. How can they be helped?

2. Self discipline

a. The most succinct definition of discipline I have come across – 'The man who can eat just one salted peanut'. The peanut attitude is invaluable and essential in leadership.

b. Field Marshal Montgomery adds, 'What advice can I give to a leader? He must discipline himself and lead a carefully regulated and ordered life. He must allow a certain time for quiet thought and reflection, and the best times are early morning, and in the evening. The quality of any action he takes, good or bad, will vary directly with the time spent in thinking.'

c. Of Dr. Sangster his son wrote: 'Time was never wasted. The difference between one minute and two was of considerable consequence to him.'

3. Use of time

a. It is usually impossible for a leader to set a regular daily timetable due to a thousand and one unexpected legitimate interruptions either by night or by day. Your priorities should be:

- Your time with the Lord personally.
- Your time with the Lord as a married couple.
- Your time with the children.
- Time for reflection and thought upon
  - immediate activities
  - personal interviews
  - spiritual ministries

135

b. Correspondence with missionaries on other stations should have the same priority as a missionary who can speak to you at any time on your own station.

4. Discipline of food and sleep

a. The body is too closely related to the soul and spirit to be ignored. Mental alertness and physical fitness count positively in our spiritual life and ministry.

b. Overweight is an unnecessary enemy in our spiritual conflict bringing heart strain, tiredness and tension. It is not difficult to find what you should weigh for your age/height. A disciplined control of the carbohydrate intake should be the answer. A 24-hour fast once a week can be remedial and inspirational as well – but it takes discipline.

c. Sleep is God's precious gift to mankind, and we cannot neglect it but at a cost. Tiredness opens the door to stress and edginess with their resultant dangers. What period of sleep is sufficient for one is not necessarily sufficient for all. Each person will have come to know the minimum – and that period of sleep should not be jeopardised too often.

5. Interruptions

Rev. J. Oswald Sanders, [the then] General Director of the Overseas Missionary Fellowship, shared a most helpful attitude learnt by a very busy man:

Up to some time ago, he testified, *I was always annoyed by interruptions which was really a form of selfishness on my part. That used to bother me. Then the Lord convinced me that God sent people my way. He sent Philip to the Ethiopian eunuch. He sent Barnabas to Saul. The same applies today; God sends people our way.*

So when someone comes in I say, 'The Lord must have brought you here. Let us find out why He sent you. Let us have prayer

136

about it!' Well, this does two things. It puts the interview on a different level because we brought God into it. Also, it generally shortens the interview. If a person knows you are looking for a reason under God why he is there, and he doesn't have one, he soon leaves for greener pastures. So take interruptions from the Lord; then they belong to your schedule. To the alert leader interruptions are only divinely-injected opportunities.

6. Discipline of rest

Let us be honest – most of us on the field work seven days a week. God did not give us the rest day in seven because it happened to be spare! So much of the strain and pressure missionaries collect is because no time is allowed for it to ebb away in relaxation. There is nothing admirable or commendable about a seven-day slog that will eventually catch up with you and adversely affect those who work with you.

Jesus dismissed the crowds – needy crowds, no doubt sick and afflicted. But He had no other recourse for renewal of His spiritual resources from the Father. It was a personal discipline to dismiss the crowd.

7. Interviewing

a. Always chat informally to begin with to put the person at ease.
b. Have prayer touching the matter of main importance.
c. Sit with light falling on the interviewee's face to catch every shade of expression.
d. Make sure you have done your homework and have all relevant books/letters, etc., to hand.
e. Seek to identify yourself with the other person so as to be fully sympathetic to his/her feelings at that moment.
f. Anything and everything can be said *in love*!
g. Interview without preconceived prejudices. Be prepared for new facts that vitally change the situation as you knew it at the beginning.

h. Never offer false assurances like, 'It will soon be all right; don't worry.' This usually creates doubt about your ability to help.

i. Avoid flat-footed pointed questions. People are often very sensitive about their lives. Guide the conversation so that this information comes out naturally.

j. Do not ask questions that can be answered 'yes' or 'no'.

k. Suspicious and accusing questions arouse suspicion and division.

l. Often, opening remarks give the clue how much confidence the interviewee has in you, or a reluctance to go deeply into the problem. His concluding remarks are also noteworthy for they will sum up what the interview has meant to him.

m. Finish the interview with prayer.

8. Communication

a. Obtain and keep close communication with each member of the field – you with the men, and your wife with the women.

b. In a field of small geographical area, personal contact ought to be once every two months. It is easier to get to grips with problems, see difficulties, hear dissatisfactions while in personal contact, rather than in the conference atmosphere. If the field is large in area, then once every four months is the minimum contact.

c. A monthly field news bulletin is essential on every field to cement cohesion, relationships, et cetera.

d. Do not hesitate to bring any to headquarters for refreshment when you observe a failure to effectively carry the load or they have done so a long time without respite.

e. Do not make yourself so busy that you have no time to keep contact with your workers.

f. People are more important than projects.

g. New workers should know you are approachable and *see* opportunities to chat with you. Make yourself available.

h. Do reply to required questionnaires sent out by the International Office or other leader needing information.

i. Keep up a regular report to all sending bases sharing news, personnel needs, project needs, and positive items of praise.

j. Keep up communication by visit and invitation with neighbouring missions.

k. Read 'Leadership' material (and apply).

9. Conferences

Before conference:

a. Two months before conference all should be invited to contribute any matter to the agenda.

b. The full agenda should be in everyone's possession at least one month before the conference, if a prayerful contribution from the field is desired. Background notes on the agenda are useful to help participants understand the problem.

c. Give *ample* time for the conference. Do not be bound to a short-time limit.

[See Chapter 17 for involvement of field committee.]

At conference:

d. It is recommended that a whole day of prayer and worship in fellowship be spent at the beginning of the conference rather than limited daily devotions.

e. It sounds hard, but experience recommends that young children are not brought to the conference room. Arrangements should be made for their care during conference hours, or mother/ father take alternate turns to the sessions.

f. Take up difficult matters when the conference is fresh – not early afternoon or late at night!

g. Always follow a hard lengthy item with a couple of short easier matters. It relieves the concentration and gives psychological lift that the conference is 'moving'.

h. Never push a conference in deadlock! Drop the matter after prayer and take up later – allow one complete session between if possible. You will find time and unofficial talks between sessions often move the log-jam.

i. Always halt a deadlock of disunity as in h., and do it again and again on the same issue if needs be. Give God time.

j. Remember to deal with moral matters in a selected Personnel Committee and report to conference the minimum necessary.

k. In matters relating to any person present, have a period with them present to ask/answer questions, then a period after they have been requested to leave the conference room.

l. All members should be warned – on each occasion – of the confidential nature of matters raised when anyone is out of the conference room, and that no information be leaked to them later.

m. Never drag meetings on later than 9–9.30 at night. Tired, weary people are in no state to maintain interest or fulfil the responsibility of finding the Lord's will when they are fighting the weariness of the flesh.

n. Watch closely, very closely, for herrings – red or any other colour. Check in your mind if the contributions are relevant to the issue – keep bringing the conference back to the point.

o. Unanimity is possible if *time* is allowed.

After the conference:

p. Copy of the official conference record to be in the hands of each member of the field within *one month*.

q. Schedule a few days immediately following the conference to complete all correspondence and fulfil the office work that has resulted from the conference.

10. Family life

a. Try and give time daily or weekly exclusively for your children.

b. If you promise the children this time let *nothing* take it away, even if important visitors arrive. They can wait, or you can excuse yourself and suggest a time later for their return. Tell your visitors why! They'll admire you all the more.

c. Never talk about fellow missionaries, or personnel related to the work, before children.

d. When children grow up, begin to share your involvement in the work. Ask their opinion about any decision that affects the whole family.

e. One rebellious 'M.K.' said, 'My father has never bought me a new dress but he can get a new tape-recorder.' A gift now and again outside anniversaries means so much. Especially when on tour ... send regular picture-cards, bring home a curio for each of them.

f. A family who prays together usually stays together!

g. Share everything with your wife. Accept no confidence that requests your wife be left outside of the knowledge shared.

h. Talk together; have time together chatting and praying.

If others are in the house:

i. Do not over-expose your family life to others. Give as much consideration to their privacy and facilities as you would to your own family.

j. Do not expect or take it for granted that 'miss' missionaries are your baby-sitters. A concern for their comfort will create a concern in them for yours.

k. At all times be tidy! I am amazed at the number of our missionary families that are content with dirty, untidy rooms and very dubious table manners, so *be manner conscious.*

11. For the woman behind the leader

a. Your husband – God's, first

Leadership makes many demands, claims, inroads on a husband's life, and often it imposes danger. It is a good thing for a wife to have a healthy fear lest unwillingness, selfishness or lack of courage should frustrate God's purposes.

A husband is a trust from God through whom He will fulfil His purposes.

b. Harmony

It is essential to maintain a harmony in one's partnership, and a unity of purpose and vision.

Any disquiet of your spirit must be shared honestly and faithfully. If your husband still feels his directive is right, then your role is in prayer. When the thought is launched into action it is for the wife to give whole-hearted support.

If a very personal matter is disturbing you, it is essential to keep sensitive as to *when* to share it with your husband. Remember he may also be experiencing as much as he can take.

Community living can be demanding on your own relationship with your husband, admiring him from a distance much of the time. To be over-demonstrative of your affection in front of others is in poor taste, and often a wounding to single workers of the fellowship. Some have known broken engagements at the cost of following Jesus thus far.

c. About family life

Often when a child behaves abominably in company, or makes repeated rude interruptions, it is because the poor child can take no more. Adults always receive priority consideration and we are insensitive to the child's deep need of attention. This creates insecurity through the upheavals and it is not easy to handle.

A few rules strictly adhered to creates a happier atmosphere than many restrictions held too loosely.

d. About counselling

When the occasion arises that for an individual's or a fellowship's sake some matter has to be honestly and frankly shared, trust the Spirit to give you clear specific facts upon which to build. One may need at times to be almost brutally blunt to get the point across. It is the human in us that would soften the blow and camouflage the issue, and this only leaves bewilderment and confusion.

12. Handling changeover in leadership

When you are appointed to succeed another

The problems are not acute when you follow another who was not a founder-leader. But even here your regime should commence with care and much grace. Not often in modern times do folk say, 'The mantle has fallen upon you.' The fact of the matter is, you have got to weave your own mantle day by day in the full glare of publicity. Personal relationship and trouble shooting, projects and vision, add thread by thread to the mantle you will wear day in and day out for no doubt several years.

New brooms sweep clean. You may have felt deeply the weaknesses of your previous leader and now is the time to build and strengthen the gaps. Go carefully. The whole field is praying for you, but they are human and are fearful of the 'wielding of the broom' that may sweep away trusted paths and relationships. Talk with others. Feel the field pulse and move lovingly and graciously but firmly where action is necessary.

When another is succeeding you

If you feel definitely it is God's time to conclude your appointment then graciously and firmly adhere to your decision. Human nature is such that difficult decisions can easily be postponed, and little conscientious application given to seek a replacement if you agree to carry on. Do not delay God's answer by yielding to an extended period. Remember if you had died, a successor would have had to be appointed!

a. The period of handing over is really determined by the seniority and experience of your successor. (Has he been at any time a deputy leader or not?)

b. In the event of a senior and experienced worker taking over, then two weeks to a month should be budgeted for him being with you on the HQ station. Should your successor be a younger man with much less experience, then a period of at least three months is indicated.

c. Systematically draw up a list of all matters that will need explanation such as:

- files.

- finance and accounts, changing Bank signatures, etc.

- properties.

- government matters and relationships. (Inform Government of new representative.)

- personnel on field and on home leave.

- new workers expected soon.

- various ministries on the field.

- field transport.

- inventory of mission properties, equipment.

- details and instructions regarding your own personal property that you may leave temporarily.

d. Before your successor arrives, systematically go through all files and destroy correspondence and material that has ceased to be relevant.

e. Go through confidential files to check all is suitable to hand over.

f. Balance all accounts, check cash balances in station and bank and hand over. Successor to sign the balance/cash as being correct.

g. Then go through the list as above, sharing relevant matters on your heart and offer advice – *not instructions* – how to continue. Go through each file summarising contents.

h. Allow plenty of time for questions.

i. In a two-week take over, the second week should see your successor in the 'hot seat' and you available as he requires and asks for assistance. Don't breathe down his neck and don't be too far away so that you are on call at any time – this is important.

j. In a three-month take-over period, the last month should see your successor operating executively with you quietly on 'stand-by'.

k. Remember God gives the anointing and lifts the anointing in accord with our appointed responsibilities. So vision and direction will be coming to 'No. 2' even as you hand over. He may differ from you on occasions, but share faithfully all the pros and cons and leave him to God and the Holy Spirit. Remember constantly your attitudes and reactions when you took over – it is very salutary to do so!

Questions for study and discussion

1. 'Leadership is largely a matter of training.' Evaluate this statement in the light of:

   a. your own experiences.

   b. your evaluation of another leader's development whom you have observed.

2. In the light of Len's comments about the value and nature of the wife's contribution (see 1f, 10f,g,h, 11a,b) discuss these with your wife and elicit her reaction.

   Is there room for improvement here?

   or, for single leaders (who have co-leaders or assistant leaders): Evaluate your relationship with your co-leaders or assistant leader.

   Are you making full use of his/her capacities? Consider discussing your relationship together.

3. 'People are more important than projects.' However, many projects directly involve people. What is your comment on Len's priority?

Bibliography

P. Wraight, *On to the Summit* (Life story of Leonard Moules), (Alresford Hants: Christian Literature Crusade, and Eastbourne, UK: Kingsway, 1981)

Note: As this chapter includes widely varied topics, the relevant bibliography is given after the chapters dealing with these topics.

SECTION V

ADMINISTRATION

15

Time Management

While it is right to recognise that our cultural background largely determines our attitude to the use of time, and that there is a vast difference between Western and Asian/African/Latin views on this, the factual 'bottom line' is that a normal waking day consists of 950-1000 minutes, and from a theological perspective, we have time for everything God wants us to do.

We need a right balance between bondage to the clock and indifference to it. God can give us this.

From another perspective our problem is really not how we handle time but how we handle ourselves. Consider this chapter as a treatment of *self-management*.

Here are some practical issues:

1. Assess every proposed activity in the light of its contribution to accepted goals.

This presupposes the hard work of considering and adopting goals.

There will be *personal* goals, *team* goals, *family* goals. There will be *immediate* goals, *intermediate* goals, and *long-term* goals.

If these are in place, in your mind, and most importantly, *in your diary*, they enable you to:

a. *Respond* to legitimate demands (because they are in line with your purpose).

b. *Refuse* (because they simply do not fit in with your God-given objectives).

148

c. *Relegate* (the demands are valid but not of high priority and can be taken care of later).

As Dwight Eisenhower once said: 'The strategic is seldom urgent and the urgent is seldom strategic.'

2. Capitalise on your strengths

a. Flow with your gifts. You will not become weary working with your gifts. You get weary operating outside your gifts. If possible delegate such tasks to those thus gifted.

b. Do the most important tasks at a time of day when you are at your maximum efficiency.

c. Allow pressure to produce maximum efficiency but avoid over-stress leading to inefficiency. (See Chapter 13 on Stress.)

3. Some practical hints

a. Set realistic deadlines and work to them.

b. Have daily recreative exercise.

c. If working on a Sunday, compensate with time off during the week.

d. Each day, list the tasks to be done in order of importance. Work steadily at them. You will have interruptions, and some items will take longer than budgeted, but stick to the system and you will be making good use of time.

e. Learn to do two things at once, such as driving and listening to a useful cassette, or working on tomorrow's list while waiting for someone.

f. Have the right equipment and use it.

g. A high percentage of a leader's time goes into communication, i.e. 1. Listening, 2. Reading, 3. Speaking, 4. Writing. Discover ways of speeding up ii. and iv., e.g. speed reading, phoning rather than writing, dictaphone, wise use of a secretary.

h. Set aside uninterruptible times for special purposes, e.g. Friday afternoon to clear a backlog of correspondence. During this time you let it be known you are not available.

i. Don't set schedules that are too tight. Interruptions always arise. So if you leave some slack time, you will be more at ease to handle the interruptions.

j. Don't become so time-conscious and work-orientated that people stay away from you. Approachability is more valuable than mere efficiency. Leaders who are 'driven' put people off.

k. If necessary, schedule into your diary recreational times with your wife and family so that you can say to anyone, 'I'm sorry; that time is already committed.'

l. Don't let your priorities be determined by what you like to do. Put the most important things first.

m. Conduct a review of your use of time in order to discover how you actually use it and what proportions of available time go to different activities. This is best done by keeping a record over several typical days of how you used each 15-minute segment.

4. Avoid these time-wasters

a. Day-dreaming.

b. Indecision.

c. Socialising.

d. Lack of goals and deadlines.

e. Not knowing where you have put it.

f. Failure to listen.

g. Fuzzy priorities.

h. Using sleep time for work and vice versa.

i. Unorganised desk/room/workspace.

j. Ignoring symptoms of a physical problem that is reducing your efficiency.

k. Working where you can be easily distracted or interrupted.

5. Overwork and workaholism (see also chapter on Stress.)

Work can be used as a means of avoiding another (undesirable) activity or responsibility; it can be an escape mechanism. Overwork takes us into the realm of the 'flesh'. You can't overwork 'in the Spirit'! Spiritual objectives are rarely accomplished by overwork. Overwork ignores God's order and man's need, and to continue in 'overload' diminishes spiritual vitality.

The most likely type of leader to overwork is the one who finds desk work more amenable than personal relationships.

6. The need for constant vigilance

Constant pressure can result in leaders getting into habits that are not conducive to effective leadership ministry.

It is strongly advocated that leaders have a *'think-tank'* with themselves at regular intervals.

This is a time of detached unhurried reflection in which the following questions may be usefully asked:

a. Am I being fair to my family?

b. Am I getting into bad time-use habits?

c. Am I getting adequate sleep?

d. Have recent events highlighted any weaknesses in my leadership pattern/style?

e. Am I generally working in line with my goals? (When were they last reviewed?)

f. Am I 'recharging the battery'? (reading, rest, recreation, retreat).

Gordon MacDonald, in *Ordering Your Private World*, says:

Time must be properly budgeted for the gathering of inner strength and resolve in order to compensate for weaknesses when spiritual warfare begins.

g. How are my relationships:
- with committee members?
- with team members?
- especially with new workers?

h. Can I easily answer the question: 'Why am I doing what I'm doing?'

i. Am I carrying excess baggage?

j. What changes do I need to make?

Another possibility is a *think-tank* with a number of close colleagues. The key here for the leader is to be seen as vulnerable and open to suggestions. Colleagues need to be encouraged to express themselves frankly. And discussions can cover a wide range of topics, not just the leader's performance.

7. Reactive or anticipatory?

The reactive lifestyle means that very little is planned; life consists of reacting to situations. Short-term solutions dominate, and life becomes a round of troubleshooting, moving from crisis to crisis.

The anticipatory lifestyle foresees needs, problems, outcomes and takes appropriate action beforehand. It thinks ahead and has a strategy; it works out ways and means of moving steadily to accepted goals.

Questions for study and discussion

1. Is there habitual misuse of time that you are conscious of, and need to correct?

2. Are your wife and family happy with the time you spend with them?

3. What do you do to recharge batteries?

4. How do you handle the assertion: 'There's just too much to do!'

5. How can you help team members in their use of time?

Bibliography

E. Dayton, *Tools for Time Management* (Grand Rapids, MI: Zondervan, 1974)

T. Engstrom and A. MacKenzie, *Managing Your Time* (Grand Rapids, MI: Zondervan, 1968)

T. Engstrom and D. Juroe, *The Work Trap* (Old Tappan, NJ: Fleming Revell, 1979)

G. MacDonald, *Ordering Your Private World* (Nashville, TN: Oliver Nelson, 1984)

16

Making Decisions

1. The leader and personal decision making

In the life of a leader there will always be the inescapable and constant necessity to make decisions. Not only is the quality of these decisions vital to the success of his ministry, there is also the issue of deciding who, because of the nature of the issue, should be involved in the decision making. This becomes a matter of value judgement.

Obviously many decisions will be made on a purely personal basis, but consultation with his deputy and/or nearby committee member or members may be wise – particularly when personnel issues are involved. A more serious matter may necessitate the calling of the committee together. A great deal will also depend on logistics – time involved, distance, expense, urgency.

A word of advice. Don't be immobilised by the fear of making a wrong decision. Every decision is a risk and it is one of the hazards of being a leader.

By all means consult, gather information, study the issue from every angle, pray; but one has to recognise that there will be a time when a decision must be made. According to a study carried out by the Laboratory of Psychological Studies in Hoboken, N.J., inability to make decisions is one of the main reasons for failure in leadership. As Prof. David Moore has said, 'The administrator's loneliest hours are spent in choosing, not between right and wrong, but between two rights.'

2. The checklist

We now proceed to the matter of trying to reduce decision making to a system. The checklist which follows can be used for either personal, small-group or team-wide decisions.

Of course it is recognised that many decisions are of a routine or minor nature for which a slavish point-by-point compliance is unnecessary. But there will be important and crucial matters where this system will prove very helpful.

a. Define exactly the situation and the limits of the situation that have produced the demand for a decision. (e.g. In accepting candidate Bloggs, the staff should be considering his suitability and readiness for the task for which he is applying – *not* whether he has developed fast in recent times, or whether the field is justified in wanting someone for that job, or whether his home church can support him.)

b. How does the situation relate to agreed objectives and will a right decision enhance the possibility of achieving them?

c. Is *all* the information needed available? Is anything being assumed? Is it an issue in which obtaining expert advice would increase the likelihood of making a right decision?

d. Are there others who could be consulted, whose experience and wise counsel would contribute to making a good decision?

e. Is there anything in print that could shed light on the area of the decision? A manual? An agreed policy? A part of *Principles and Practice*? A field/base bye-law? An international guideline? An international conference report? Special research?

f. Can you recall a similar situation and how it was handled? Can that teach anything about how to handle this?

g. *Pray* (in the sense of spreading the matter before God, seeking the illumination of the Holy Spirit regarding the way forward and deliverance from wrong motives. See point k.).

h. Formulate all possible alternative decisions which contribute to the achievement of agreed objectives and meet the demands of the situation.

i. Invite discussion with a view to evaluating the consequences – positive and negative – of each alternative in point h.

j. Tentatively decide on the course of action which has the most positives and least negatives, or, if it is a group decision, the course of action about which a consensus view exists.

k. Check that the decision

- has not been subject to any of these pressures: tradition, change for change's sake, forceful personalities, keeping the peace, fear of consequences, dogmatism, cultural, as distinct from biblical, demands, and

- has these qualities: fair, ethical, scriptural, conducive to good fellowship.

l. Seek in prayer for the witness of the Spirit as a confirmation of the rightness of the decision (see Colossians 3:15). If this is present, proceed to stage m. If not, go back to point h. and re-examine the alternatives.

m. Make the decision and implement it by assigning responsibilities for action. Provide such information as needed for all parties involved.

n. Establish a review time and mechanism to check on:

- the rightness of the decision, and

- the correctness of its execution, in the sense that progress is made towards the end in view.

o. Review progress at the time set in the previous point above and be ready to make adjustments.

No attempt has been made in the preceding checklist to give advice on the progress or handling of the discussion. The goal has been simply to provide a foolproof checklist and to ensure that no significant factor is omitted from consideration.

3. Procedural matters – group decisions

Here are a number of additional points which will enhance the likelihood of a smooth discussion leading to a right decision and effective follow-through.

a. Where a whole team is involved in a major issue, it is good for each member to be given as much advance notice of the discussion as possible. (It is unwise to 'drop' an issue on the team at conference and expect an instant decision.)

b. If possible the committee should have a preliminary discussion and be able to bring alternative proposals to the group (preferably ahead of the discussion, although this may not be possible).

c. The understanding of alternative proposals will be made easier if each person has a printed copy of them beforehand, or if they can be written up on an overhead projector or blackboard during the discussion.

d. The leader of the discussion should be open for questions and for contributions 'from the floor' – provided they are relevant to the main discussion. Avoid tangents by firmly keeping speakers to the issue under discussion.

e. The crucial stage is when a consensus is beginning to emerge. It is important that this should not be derailed or thwarted by individuals who have an axe to grind – a 'hidden agenda'.

It is also important for the leader to be able to articulate the emerging consensus in a way that will foster the flow of united thinking.

f. If, after a reasonable amount of time, no consensus seems to be emerging, do not 'force the pace'. It is better to leave it and return to it later in the conference, with an appeal for earnest prayer, both on the spot as a group, and privately during the intervening time.

g. Sometimes a 'word from the Lord' comes through a member and it is not in line with previous thinking or proposals. If it is from God it will have the mark of the Spirit about it, and sensitive team members will recognise it. The leader must be ready to pick this up and move with it even though it cuts across other plans. The goal is not to win an argument but discern the Lord's purpose.

h. Agreement should be reached regarding who will be responsible for any review further down the track, and what authority this group will have to make mid-course corrections.

i. Always ensure that those who will be part of the implementation are part of the decision making. And if someone who is going to be affected is unavoidably absent from the discussion, do not finalise until they can be consulted.

j. Do not let the conference 'nit-pick' on the exact wording of a resolution. Appoint a small group to work on it and bring a written proposal.

Questions for study and discussion

1. Why do we find it easier to analyse and evaluate, rather than decide?

2. What issues were at stake in these two decision-making episodes: Numbers 13:26-14:12 and 1 Kings 18:16-20?

3. Some have found that the major problem has not been the making of a decision but the implementation of it. If this has been your experience, study the reasons why.

4. What place should faith have in decision making?

Bibliography

C. Kepner & B. Tregoe, *The Rational Manager* (A systematic approach to problem solving and decision making.) (New York, USA: McGraw Hill, 1965)

L. Schaller, *The Decision Makers* (Nashville, TN: Abingdon, 1974)

A three-stage decision-making process

STAGE I

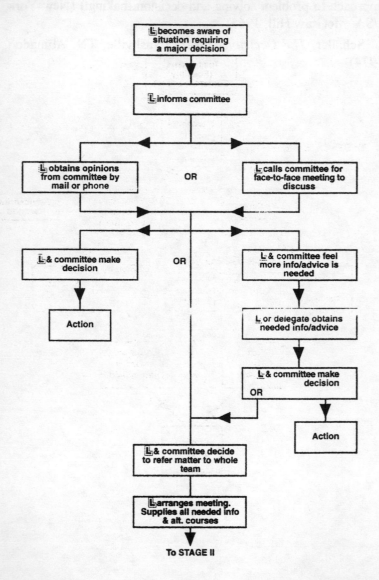

L becomes aware of situation requiring a major decision

↓

L informs committee

↓

L obtains opinions from committee by mail or phone — **OR** — L calls committee for face-to-face meeting to discuss

↓

L & committee make decision — **OR** — L & committee feel more info/advice is needed

↓

Action

L or delegate obtains needed info/advice

↓

L & committee make decision — **OR**

↓

Action

L & committee decide to refer matter to whole team

↓

L arranges meeting. Supplies all needed info & alt. courses

To STAGE II

STAGE II

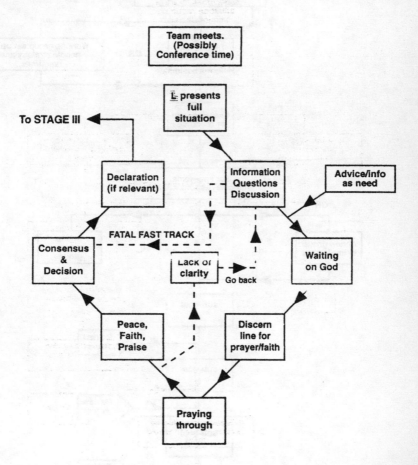

Team meets.
(Possibly
Conference time)

L presents
full
situation

To STAGE III

Declaration
(if relevant)

Information
Questions
Discussion

Advice/info
as need

FATAL FAST TRACK

Consensus
&
Decision

Lack of
clarity

Go back

Waiting
on God

Peace,
Faith,
Praise

Discern
line for
prayer/faith

Praying
through

STAGE III (relevant if decision relates to goals, strategy, policy)

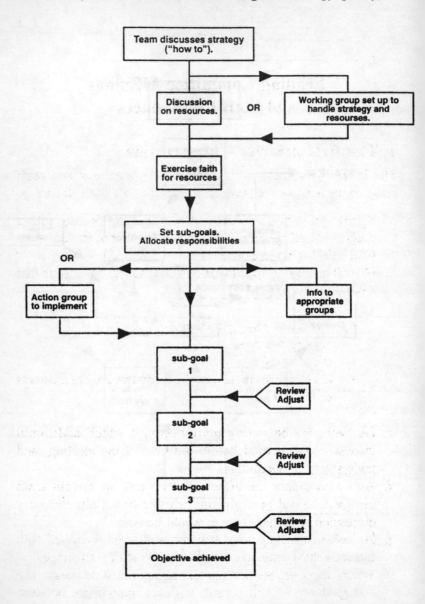

17

Leading Committee Meetings and Staff Conferences

1. The first priority – preparation

The secret of success both in committee meetings and staff conferences is *adequate preparation* on the part of the leader.

a. During preceding weeks/months he will be putting into a special file all the topics that need discussion and decision, with relevant correspondence.

b. He will be making specific daily prayer targets of matters that have the potential for:

   - increasing team effectiveness.
   - causing friction.
   - occasioning change.
   - affecting in a crucial way the life and ministry of members of the team.

c. He will also be noting matters about which additional information is needed before the time of the meeting, and taking steps to obtain this.

d. As he considers the effect of decisions on certain team members he will be evaluating whether or not a preliminary discussion with these people would be wise.

e. He will be deciding what matters need to be discussed with the committee prior to going before the staff conference.

f. Where there are serious matters about which he needs help and guidance he will consult with the appropriate persons, e.g. deputy leader, senior workers, Regional Secretary, or International Office personnel.

g The leader will do all he can to give prior notice of agenda items so that participants have time for thought and prayer.

2. Points specifically relating to a committee meeting

This is a smaller and, possibly, less formal meeting than a full staff conference and lends itself to in-depth discussion of crucial matters.

a. The leader can use it as a sounding board for tentative ideas.

b. The leader can use it as a means of discovering attitudes and values of the group as a whole. This can be a guiding factor in formulating proposals and policy.

c. The leader needs to be evaluating what matters can be finalised within the committee and what need to go to the total fellowship. (Some sensitive personnel matters, especially moral issues, should not be discussed in open conference.)

d. The committee can examine exhaustively various alternative propositions and come up with guidelines that will be useful to the general conference.

e. In important matters that need conference decisions the committee must avoid giving the impression that issues have been decided beforehand. Conference should not be a rubber stamp affair.

f. Committee members (or even rank-and-file members) can be asked to do additional research on a topic before conference or a small working group may be formed for such a purpose.

g. Although less formal it is crucial that the decisions of the committee be minuted and approved before members disperse.

h. The committee should not deliberate on matters that should be treated at a lower level (i.e. department/ ministry/station level).

3. Points that relate to staff conferences

a. Why have Conferences?

It might be valuable to discuss first the question: 'Why have a staff conference?' Basically, the history of WEC once Norman Grubb returned from Zaire and became British Secretary has been the history of staff conferences. They were quarterly for many years and every staff member was free to attend.

As the group grew, this made for slow progress in discussions, but the dictum that 'participation in decision making is the key to motivation and unity' has prevailed.

So here are some of the reasons for holding a staff conference:

- Spiritual refreshing through worship and ministry of the Word.
- Building of team unity through fellowship interaction and relaxation together.
- Motivation for continuing development of the work through participation in strategy discussions and decision making.
- Stimulation of vision and purpose through strategic input from the leader, leadership group and/or invited participants (e.g. International Office personnel).
- 'Clearing the air' of problems that may have arisen since the last meeting.
- Skill development through seminars on appropriate topics.

b. Conduct of Staff Conference

- Make prayer primary, not perfunctory. Pray through at the start, till you sense peace about proceeding. Pray if you get stuck. Commit decisions to the Lord as you make them. Break up into small groups for prayer at times. Always end sessions with prayer and praise.
- Establish the right atmosphere. This intangible factor is of supreme importance. Like it or not, it is largely established by

the leader. If you are tense, the atmosphere will be tense. If you are free in spirit about the outcome and decisions, the atmosphere will be free. If you can 'hang loose' in discussion, a joke or humorous comment will come easily and the group will sense this easy detachment. If you are known as one who is really concerned to elicit comments, the reticent will be more likely to contribute. If you are known as one who carefully evaluates all contributions, then others will feel stimulated to make a wise and productive comment.

- Have an agenda for all, or written up on a board or overhead projector. This not only ensures that all are aware of issues, but acts as a morale builder as folks are able to tick off matters dealt with; it is also a discipline factor – if members see 'so much to do' they will more likely limit contributions to the essentials.

- On introducing every topic, give sufficient background so that people fully understand the situation. Probably you will know more than anyone else. Have a thought for those who are not informed.

- Having introduced the topic, lay out the alternative courses of action, with your own evaluation of each. This will give the group 'something to chew on', and keep the discussion relevant.

- Stick to the topic and gently but firmly steer the discussion back when people introduce non-relevant material.

- All contributions should be addressed to the chairperson, but it is not good for the chairperson to respond personally to everyone. Keep the discussion flowing in the fellowship.

- Take note of reticent members and make it easy for them to participate. 'What are you thinking about this, Jean?'

- It is a recipe for chaos to say, 'What should we do about so and so?' Rather, 'There are a number of alternative ways we can handle this ...' Then the discussion will be easy to keep in order.

- Try to ensure that decisions are reached objectively and constructively, without emotion. The following are illegitimate factors in conference decision making:
    - Prejudice
    - Threats/ultimatums
    - Fear of change
    - Traditions
    - Insufficient knowledge
    - Factional spirit
    - 'Sacred cows'
    - Rivalry
    - Dominance by forceful personalities
- Ensure that tentative decisions do not contravene *Ps and P*, *International Guidelines*, field by-laws, or agreed goals and strategy.
- If deadlock is reached, terminate the discussion by a time of prayer and reschedule future discussion after private prayer.
- There is no need to follow Roberts' Book of Common Order; however, once a consensus is reached this must be minuted, read out (or printed or placed on an overhead projector) and approved by those present.
- The minute should record the *decision* not the *discussion*. (Explanatory notes can be appended for distant members, but these should not be part of the minutes.)
- When action is needed, the person/s to take the action must also be minuted, and the person informed (if not present). Areas of responsibility must be clearly defined.
- Set up small working groups if some matters need detailed analysis. Arrange a report time.
- Avoid scheduling important meetings, or at least introducing

important topics, when people are already tired; mental tiredness has more potential for trouble than physical.

See also Chapter 14 The Wisdom of Leonard Moules.

Chapter 16 Making Decisions.

Chapter 9 The Challenge of Change.

4. Some general comments on planning a staff conference

a. Discourage overnight travel before the day conference begins.

b. Spend a day in getting acquainted, ministry, sharing wider WEC information, prayer for the world of WEC, and for agenda items to be discussed.

c. Make use of suitably gifted workers to lead worship, devotional and ministry session.

d. Do not have as a first agenda item a matter of major concern. The conference needs to 'shake down' and settle into a good pattern.

e. Conference items are a golden opportunity for skill improvement programmes. Plan ahead for seminars and workshops, choosing topics relative to felt needs. Invite suitably qualified specialists if possible.

f. Consider whether chairing of sessions can be delegated. (This leaves the leader freer to participate and broadens the experience of the deputy leader or committee member.)

g. Have a time for a few hours of relaxation and informal fellowship sometime during the conference.

h. Children at conferences. Plan stimulating programmes for the MKs using outside helpers (visiting relatives, local Christians, friends from other missions, etc.) so that parents can be free to participate in conference sessions.

i. Plan for 'special interest' or regional groups or sub-teams to meet together to discuss matters specifically related to them.

j. By all means use gifted WEC personnel from other fields or bases to bring ministry, but do not be exclusive or insular. Make use of others outside of WEC whose expertise can enrich the fellowship.

k. Remember, some may be present with aching hearts, frustrated spirits, and disappointed hopes. Conference fellowship times can be a wonderful opportunity for sharing and praying for one another. These should be unhurried times under wise and discerning leadership. The awareness that the fellowship cares and identifies with a wounded worker can make all the difference between resignation and perseverance.

l. Inevitably conference time is when problem issues and administrative hassles have to be sorted out, but do not allow problem solving to take precedence over planning and strategy sessions. Firmly schedule these into the programme before commencing so that they are not crowded out.

Never let conference sessions be crowded. Extend the whole conference time if necessary, and insist that *all* attend.

Questions for study and discussion

1. In the light of current situations in your field or base what should be the goals of your next annual staff conference?

2. Review your last three annual conferences. What have been the strengths and weaknesses? What can you learn from this?

3. What can keep your team from being too insular and detached from the wider ministry of the mission?

Bibliography

S. Dinnen (Ed.), *WEC Leader's Manual* (Gerrards Cross, UK: WEC International, Undated)

18

Evaluating Your Leadership

The questionnaire below is worded in such a way that it can be used by any rank-and-file members of your team in making an assessment of your leadership.

Alternatively, it might be given to some of your senior workers or committee members.

As a final resort, it can be filled in by the leader himself, although this will probably not be totally objective!

The suggested rating is 0–5. Allot a mark and then add up, against a possible 250.

The subjects covered have been dealt with in this book.

Section 1   PASTORAL CARE   Score 0-5

1. Does L. show an active and consistent concern for your spiritual welfare?

2. Does L. evidence a real concern for your physical, emotional, financial, material welfare?

3. Does L. show a concern for your effectiveness in ministry?

4. Does L. visit sufficiently often to really understand your hassles?

5. Does L. show that he knows your spiritual gifts and is he concerned for their development?

6. Is L. encouraging you to upgrade your abilities?

7. Does L. give you sufficient scope to develop your ministry?

8. Does L. have sensitivity, vision and insight in counselling?

9. Does L. put team welfare before his own personal ministry?

Section 2   PERSONAL EXAMPLE

10. Does L. set a good example of diligence and a wise use of time?

11. Does L. give an adequate lead in faith and prayer?

12. Is L. approachable?

13. Does L. keep promises?

14. Does L. keep confidences?

15. Is L. a good listener?

16. Is L. willing to accept and consider criticism?

17. Does L. set a good example in family life and responsibility?

18. Does L. take sufficient time off to 'recharge his batteries'?

19. Does L. believe in and practise 'stretch reading'? (Books that increase ability.)

20. Does L. have a sense of humour so that people are relaxed in his presence?

Section 3   ADMINISTRATIVE SKILLS

21. Does L. delegate?

22. Does L. avoid being bogged down and overloaded by taking on non-essentials?

23. Does L. have a good sense of balance?

24. Does L. have the right priorities?

25. Is L. genuinely open to new ideas from other people?

26. Is L. fair and firm in handling difficult matters/people?

26. Is L. fair and firm in handling difficult matters/people?

27. Does L. show initiative and have fresh ideas?

28. Is L. a good motivator of others?

29. Can L. think ahead and plan wisely?

30. Can L. cope with differing viewpoints or is he defensive?

31. Does L. exercise his authority wisely?

32. Does L. react wisely in problem situations?

33. Can L. keep his cool under pressure?

34. Can L. analyse situations accurately and come up with relevant solutions?

Section 4   RELATIONSHIPS

35. Does L. relate well to team members and committee members?

36. Is L. sensitive in the fellowship area? Does he work towards building fellowship?

37. Does L. relate well to the RS (fields only)?

38. Does L. utilise the mission resources available to him? (i.e. field/base committee members, library, International Office, International Research Office, International Training and Resources Office, Inter-mission organisation)

39. Does L. maintain a good level of communication within the field/base?

40. Does L. send round useful articles, magazines, letters with improvement value?

41. Can L. make staff conferences/ committee meetings happy occasions, conducted in a relaxed atmosphere?

42. Does L. encourage all to participate in discussions, so that a true consensus is reached?

43. Is L. good at balancing concern for people as against concern for work?

172

church workers and leaders? (For Sending Base Leaders (SBL): does L. relate well to pastors and Christian leaders?)

45. Does L. have a sensitivity to national viewpoints in the work?

Section 5   MISSION AWARENESS AND LOYALTY

46. Does L. stimulate interest in and prayer for other fields/bases/ministries of WEC?

47. Does L. cultivate and encourage a good flow of information from the field to SBs? (For SBLs – a good flow from his base to fields.)

48. Does L. evidence and encourage a high regard for the organisation's principles?

49. Is information from other fields and bases circulated regularly?

50. Does L. encourage and show appreciation for visits from other fields/bases/ ministries?

TOTAL OUT OF 250

WHAT TO DO WITH THE RESULTS

The actual score is, of course, significant (although no one is suggesting resignation if it is under 125!).

It is probably more valuable to try to spot *areas* that need attention. If you emerge with a series of low scores in, say, pastoral care, or personal relationships, or administrative skills, or mission loyalty then this should become an area for prayer, study and discussion with others with a view to improvement.

One also needs to bear in mind the availability of senior workers such as the Regional Secretaries or International Office personnel who would be delighted to help you in any way they can. Leadership development is one of their highest priorities.

It should also be noted that every leadership position is different and that the particular mix of leadership skills needed will vary from situation to situation. Even within the same situation needed skills can be different at different times. For instance, in one sending base, after one somewhat charismatic and forceful leader stepped down, the team felt that a 'fellowship-builder' was needed, and elected such a person. In another situation the leader was somewhat conservative, emphasising the need for consolidation rather than advance; his successor was a person with more vision and initiative. So needs can vary in the same situation.

If you 'mean business' in the whole area of improved leadership skills, God is going to meet you and show you the way through. Be encouraged! 'The one who calls you is faithful and *he will do it*' (1 Thess. 5:24).

Where possible I detail the source of the the various quotations made in this book. However, with regard to some quotations I am not able to identify the source.

Pages 14-15: *A Theology of Church Leadership*, L. Richards and C. Hoeldtke, Grand Rapids, Zondervan 1980

Pages 17-18: *Practical Anthropology*, now out of circulation.

Page 33: Samuel Shoemaker, Source unknown.

Pages 34-35: Mike Mansfield. Source unknown.

Page 35: TIME magazine. Issue not noted.

Page 40: Richard Halverson. Source not noted.

Page 47: *Competent to Lead*. Kenneth Gangel, Moody Press, Chicago, 1974.

Page 61: Glenn Kendall, Evangelical Missions Quarterly, July, 1988.

Page 63: Peter Wiwcharuk, *Manual on Leadership* (no details).

Pages 64-65: J. Michael Kuiper, Evangelical Missions Quarterly, Oct. 1988.

Pages 76-77: Norman Grubb, *Touching the Invisible*, CLC, Fort Washington, 1987.

Page 77: Ted Engstrom, *Making of a Christian Leader*, Zondervan, 1976.

Page 85: Thomas Watson. Source unknown.

Chas. Krauthammer, TIME, date not noted.

Pages 85-86: Samuel Huntington. Source unknown.

Page 86: Mancur Olson. Source unknown.

Page 95: Samuel Mateer. Source unknown.

Pages 98-99: Noel Gibson, *Evicting Demonic Squatters and Breaking Bondages*.

Pages 102-103: Ted Engstrom. Source unknown.

Page 105: A.W. Tozer. Source unknown.

Page 108-109: Peter Drucker, *The Effective Executive*, Pan Books, London 1966

Page 119-120: John Silk, Christian Literature Crusade.

Page 120: 'How to avoid burnout', Life Ministries Magazine. PO Box 200, San Dimas, CA 91773

Page 121: K. Sehnert, *Stress/Unstress*, Augsburg, Minneapolis, 1981.

Page 122: Marjorie Foyle, *Honourably Wounded*. MARC Europe, London, 1987.

Pages 124-126: K. and M. O'Donnell EMQ Jan 1991. They quote C. Johnson and D. Penner who surveyed N. American Protestant Missions in 1981, Dorothy Gish and her survey of the same subject in 1983 and Phil Parshall in his survey of 1987.

Page 133: Alan Norris, *Christian Leadership*, Overcomer Trust, Poole.

Pages 136-137: J. Oswald Sanders. Source Unknown.

Page 151: Gordon Macdonald. *Ordering Your Private World*, Highland Books, UK